THE FATHER'S EMBRACE
The Father-Son Life

MARLON WILLIAMSON

BCG
PRESS

ISBN PRINT: 979-8-9933594-0-3
ISBN DIGITAL: 979-8-9933594-1-0

The author does not dispense advice or prescribe any aspect of mental health counsel, direction or treatment, either directly or indirectly. The author's story aims to inspire readers to identify, explore, and overcome life's challenges.

If the reader sees themselves or a personal life situation similar as the one found in this book, please see this as a coincidence. The author has used analogy or metaphor, removed names, changed certain details and particular references to ensure total anonymity to all persons.

BCG Press
Publishing Division of Brikwoo
www.brikwoo.com

Cover Design
Brian Wooten

Interior Design
Christopher Littleton

CONTENT

FOREWORDS

"The Father's Embrace," is a tremendous look into one of the greatest issues affecting our nation and the direction it is taking our children. Absent fathers have left a great void in the hearts of young men and women who will seek affirmation wherever it can be found. The cry is piercing from those who are acting out of their pain in rebellion, addictions, and a serious lack of self-esteem. An orphan spirit is at work in them and even in those who have fathers, but their fathers fail to have time to invest in their sons.

> *Hear, ye children, the instruction of a father, and attend to know understanding.* (**Proverbs 4:1KJV**)

Our Heavenly Father has laid out instruction for us as fathers to raise up our sons to walk in the purposes of God. Not only are we to impart spiritual instruction to them, but the everyday wisdom that fathers teach their sons to grow into Godly men with skills to lead his family.

This moving treatise by Bishop Marlon Williamson is an uncovering of his own heart and the pain that followed him throughout his life. The void that lived in his heart that he never understood until he found out later in life that his biological father had walked out on their family.

Bishop Williamson was able to overcome the orphan spirit the enemy had brought into his life and this has become the motivation for him to write this book. His heart is to be the father to his children both natural and spiritual that he never had. And, he has done this very well.

I have traveled to many nations with Bishop Williamson and his wife Pastor Brenda Williamson. I have seen the joy that lights up his life as he pours into children and Pastors that serve in these nations, many who have experienced and are facing the same orphan spirit he was challenged with.

I highly recommend this book and believe it holds the answers so many are searching for. It is a glorious expression of our Heavenly Fathers heart and His intention for His seed.

He is truly bringing many sons to glory!

Bishop Darrell Barber B.Th.
Author, Co-Host of Empowering Life
Ministries Podcast
Empowering Life Ministries
Lexington, Tennessee 38351
www.empoweringlifeministries.com

In a time when the crisis of fatherlessness is reshaping the soul of a nation, Bishop Marlon delivers a timely and prophetic call to action. This important book explores the irreplaceable role of fathers in shaping identity, stability, and legacy in the lives of sons and daughters—especially within the Christian community. With wisdom rooted in Scripture and the relational love of the Father, Son, and Holy Spirit, Bishop Marlon challenges the Church to reclaim and reflect the values of divine fatherhood.

As someone who has had the privilege of calling Bishop Marlon my spiritual father for the past 12 years, I can personally testify to the transformative power of his guidance, love, and example. This book is more than a message—it's a mantle. A clarion call to heal generational wounds, restore families, and raise up a generation that knows who they are and whose they are. May we return to the heart of the Father.

Peace and every good to each and all.

Pastor Kevin Gurley
Word of Life Ministry
Fort Payne, AL
www.wolministry.org

"And he shall turn the heart of the fathers to the children,
and the heart of the children to their fathers…"
Malachi 4:6 (KJV)

There is a turning taking place in this generation—a divine turning of hearts. We are witnessing both the great need and the great call for fathers to rise up and take their rightful place in the lives of their children. Not just biological fathers, but spiritual fathers too—those who will lead, teach, nurture, and affirm.

We are living in a time when the absence of a father's voice has left a wound in many. That silence has echoed loudly in the hearts of sons who wander, seeking identity, validation, and love. The cry of the orphan spirit is not just from those without fathers, but even from those whose fathers were present but never truly invested. A present body does not always equal a present heart.

In this powerful and transparent work, Bishop Marlon Williamson shares not only his testimony, but a divine invitation for healing and restoration. His journey of discovering the absence of his earthly father—and the pain that followed—has become a well-spring of healing for others. What the enemy meant to destroy him, God has used to raise him up as a father to many.

Through the grace and power of the Holy Spirit, Bishop Marlon Williamson has broken the cycle. His life bears the fruit of a man who chose to forgive, to overcome, and to love deeply. Whether natural or spiritual, his heart beats with the Father's desire—to restore sons, and to call forth fathers.

I've had the honor and privilege of traveling the nations with Bishop Marlon and Pastor Brenda. And in those adventures, I have watched Bishop Marlon carry this message not as a project, but as a mantle from our Heavenly Father. His words flow with the authority of experience and the compassion of a father's heart. My prayer is that as you read these pages, something deep within you will awaken — that the cry of the orphan spirit will be silenced by the voice of a Father who loves you unconditionally.

Let this book stir your heart and call you into restoration, reconciliation, and purpose.

Apostle Donna Barber B. Th.
Empowering Life Ministries

THE FATHER'S EMBRACE
The Father-Son Life

CHAPTER ONE

INTRODUCTION

Our world, our governments and the church are in a major reset and shifting. The heightened tensions from our political and racial debates, along with burgeoning gender and sexuality conflicts, have confronted us with ever-increasing unanswered questions. For many of us, our circumstances are in direct conflict with our convictions. We often seek simple answers to very complex questions.

When we attempt to package truth or even who God is in our neat little boxes, we are often being very naïve and possibly arrogant. Neither I, nor you, nor any other individual has a monopoly on truth or revelation. Even our valid revelations and understandings of truth are ever-increasing and expanding at best. We are looking through our individual lenses of understanding and processing everything through our own personal experience filters. That alone should encourage each of us to give grace and space for everyone to "work out" their own salvation and to trust that God will bring each along the path of life in His way and great wisdom.

As I write these words, I realize the huge difference in preaching a sermon and writing a book. Most everything in this book has come from my sermon material - messages I have delivered over the years, but preaching has many advantages. When you say something to a live audience, you have the immediate benefit of seeing or hearing their reaction. You also can discern the atmosphere in real-time. Then, you can proceed to clarify or expound further if needed. You have palpable evidence as to whether the same Spirit that stirred your soul as you delivered the Word is stirring the hearts of those who receive it. In education, they call this formative assessment - an assessment that is done during learning that allows the teacher to shift methods and approaches in order to better meet the learners' needs. Done well, it is an invaluable tool for pastors or for any public speaker. All of this is unavailable when the message is written, and the reader and the author are not in the same place at the same moment. So, as I wrote this text, I did so in hopes that it will give the reader a bit of insight into my heart. As the editing and printing are finished, no real-time dialogue or discussion is possible. I trust the Father to communicate His heart through the Holy Spirit, as only He can. And I trust the reader to give me grace to understand the earnest and overwhelming spirit of love and inclusion in which this text was written.

As we set out on this journey to fully understand our God as the Good Father and ourselves as His sons, we must attend to this term, Father, as it relates to the true and living God - Creator of all. The fact that God, Himself, chose to identify Himself as a *father* says much about the role. I do not believe this was a gender identification, but rather a revelation of His nature and purpose. That purpose was primarily to reproduce himself in a family of sons that would reveal and reflect Who He is and how He thinks. Gender identity and sexuality preferences are hot-button issues of our day, but gender issues are nothing new. We must acknowledge that the church has been complicit over the decades and centuries in fostering prejudice and divisions among the sexes, especially as they relate to spiritual authority.

While fatherless children are still, thankfully, in the minority, we are, in fact, many. Our best hope, it seems, is to become a second minority - to be one who beats the odds - to be the ones who wrestled with the demons that viciously attack a fatherless child with consistency and force and to emerge from the darkness into a place of functionality and hope. It is a journey not for the faint of heart. And while it is a journey no child would choose for himself, statistically, men whose fathers were absent when they were children are more likely to become absent fathers, themselves, and women whose fathers were absent are more likely to have children whose fathers are absent. *Truly, the rich get richer, and the poor get poorer.*

> *"For whoever has will be given more, and they will have an abundance. Whoever does not have, even what they have will be taken from them* (**Matthew 25:29, NIV**).

What a paradox this is! We would never choose this for ourselves, but something about the trauma of the journey threatens not only us, but our children and our children's children. The generational grip is tight, and its sinister whispers, dark and discouraging, somehow reach our ears not only in childhood but throughout the course of our lives.

It is with the echoes of that voice in mind that I write this book.

These ears of mine have heard (and even entertained) those whispers. I write this book because, in truth, I personally have wrestled, grappled, and triumphed over, only to wrestle again with this imposing and accusing shadow of fatherlessness.

I've been on this journey for the whole of my life - as a lost son, a rebellious son, an orphan, an immature son, a young father, an older father, a spiritual father, and now a grandfather (Papa) to five beautiful grandkids. I have experienced the ups and downs, the joys, and heartaches of all these seasons of life. After all these years of parenting, pastoring and business life, I felt the compelling call to write and to find a deeper why to my life purpose, and I came up with a pretty good life statement:

I want to be a catalyst for generational influence.

Once I had penned this statement, I percolated on it, both content with its embodiment of my mission and aware that its roots grow much deeper. Conscious of the importance of those roots, I began to dig deeper - to seek out the seed of this powerful drive. I discovered that the underlying reasons for these desires are as powerful as the drive they create, if not more so. When I understand why I have this passion for generational guidance, I fully understand the implications of both sides of this issue, and if I am going to break the cycle so that I can be the father my children need, the grandfather my grandchildren need, and the spiritual father to anyone, I must first be the seeking son. I must first understand the value of what I didn't have if I am to establish it in my life today.

The process of coming to the root of my dedication to this work involved using a root cause analysis strategy that was first developed and used by Sakichi Toyoda - a strategy called *The Five Whys* (NexGen). I began by asking myself why this statement was so important to me, and when I came to the answer to that question, I asked why that answer was true, and I repeated the question again and again until I got to the answer that was powerful enough that it did not need another question. All of the answers are significant, but the final answer is, I believe, the true seed of the call to this work. Consider my process:

Root Cause / Reason Inquiry

Why is being a catalyst for generational influence important?
Because I do not want to come and go in this world and not have any lasting evidence that my purpose was fulfilled.

Why is this important - that I have lasting evidence of the fulfillment of my purpose?
Because I have lived my life with little to no spiritual heritage.

Why is the fact that I have lived my life with little or no spiritual heritage important?
Because I have struggled my entire life searching for affirmation and identity as a son and now as a father.

Why is this struggle - why is this search - so important?
Because I do not want my heirs, natural and spiritual, to wander through their lives with unanswered questions, insecurities, self-doubt and wounded orphan hearts.

My hope for this text is that it reaches someone who is in need of its message and for whom it will bring hope, for whom it will remove the shame and frustration that hold so many in the prison of an identity crisis. If we do not know who we are created to be, the world around us will offer up its best opinion. If we receive that opinion, we run the risk of living a lie. It is only when we discover the original, good plan the Father has for us and begin to trust the pattern which He provided that we will live a life of peace, joy and fulfillment.

I embarked on this journey as a child much in need of a father and grew into a boy who caught glimpses of what fatherhood could be from watching the fathers of friends and their empowering interactions. These observations fed me powerful ideas about what it would mean to be a son to that kind of father. These were just ideas - slippery specters of hope that I couldn't quite hold onto. And then it happened. As a young man I found myself suddenly and unexpectedly facing the role of fatherhood myself, and it rocked me to my core. This idea of fatherhood - these shards of images and ideas I had loosely joined together, like a teetering piece of folk art, dangling piece-to-piece - would now become concrete. And though I was in no way ready for it, I knew - somehow I absolutely knew - that this was *my* role, *my* responsibility. What I didn't realize at the time was that it would be, perhaps, my most significant *calling* in life.

It was a pivotal moment in my life, for which I will always be grateful. And while I didn't fully understand that at the time, somehow, I could see enough light to know that I must embrace it - must secure the pieces of the folk-art-sculpture together, must bring them to stability, resculpt, re-form, build and sand and perfect this vision of true fatherhood so that I could step into that vision - so that I could become, not the kind of father I had, but the kind of father I'd always needed. The one I spent my childhood wondering about. And in that journey - in the becoming, I found healing. In the becoming, I heard the voice of God. I feel I must make one more point before I go forward. All along this journey with the hearing of God's voice, the healing and the gifts of His grace and guidance, I received these not as a son of God, but as a child of God. The scriptures are full of paradox - as are we - as is God, Himself (Themselves). As we were made not in His image, but in Their image, after Their likeness.

Gender is a powerfully important part of who we are and of how we were made. It would be an error, indeed, to negate the beauty and power that are at the core level of gender for each of us. And at the same time, as we were created in the image of God, we know that God sees, loves and calls us in equity and in honor to the diversity in which we were created. And we know that that diversity exists in the "they" of the triune God - that the feminine would not exist in us if the feminine did not exist in Them. And so truth and calling and healing are for all - without respect of gender - or ethnicity - of economic status - of education level - or of any other thing. I believe the messages within this text are for us all.

In the course of this text, I use masculine language frequently. For one thing, I am a man who was abandoned by his father at an early age and who sought and still seeks to become a strong father to his own children. My perspective is masculine.

Additionally, much of the language of the scriptures is masculine. When we use language and words such as *father, fatherhood, son,* and *sonship,* it can easily begin to look like an exclusionary list. What about mothers, motherhood and daughters? While it is not practical for me to fully address the gender equity and equal opportunity issues of our world in this writing, I do want to make some things as clear as possible as they pertain to the intentions of this text.

God is not prejudiced or biased. God is neither exclusively male nor female. God is not sexist. God is not a bigot. God has no respect of persons. In the Kingdom of God, there are no second-class citizens or spiritual stepchildren. Christ transcends our sexual differences. I say all this to say that God the Father is Spirit. Christ is spirit. The idea of spiritual fathers and sons has nothing to do with gender. I have heard the voice of the Father many times through the vessel of a woman. I have witnessed the love of the Father expressed through many women. I have witnessed the ministry of Christ and the Holy Spirit through many women. It is not a gender issue; it is a spiritual matter.

> So then, from now on, we have a new perspective
> that refuses to evaluate people merely by their outward
> appearances. For that's how we once viewed the Anointed
> One, but no longer do we see him with limited human
> insight. Now, if anyone is enfolded into Christ, he has
> become an entirely new creation. All that is related to the
> old order has vanished. Behold, everything is fresh and new
> (**2 Corinthians 5:16-17, TPT**).

Throughout the entire process of writing and reviewing the content of this book, it became more clear than ever that there are many who have been wounded, abused and disillusioned by some who have used much of the same language, principles and titles I include in this writing. I am aware of the *shepherding* movement and some *sonship* movements of the past that took many of these same ideas to an extreme, controlling, and fear-based doctrine. I am also aware that many have guarded hearts that have been wounded in so many different ways by so-called *spiritual* fathers.

If you are among those who have been abused, neglected, shamed or wounded in any way by those who should have nurtured and cared for you, please allow me to ask for your forgiveness on behalf of the fathers and spiritual leaders who failed you. I pray that in some way this message can help you find your healing and connection to the Father.

Many years ago, I heard the story of how banks would train their tellers to spot counterfeit bills. The key was to study the authentic bills, not the fake ones. Counterfeits come in many forms and change over time, but as long as you know the truth, you can always spot a lie. Money is used everyday for corrupt uses and abuses, but we do not throw away our money, do we? This has been a profound element of my search - watching good fathers, considering their actions, their motives, their words. Eaves-dropping on father-son interactions with my friends. Noticing the good - not in bitterness for what I lacked, but in the spirit of curiosity and potential for application toward my own spiritual growth. In the same spirit, I simply ask that you open your heart and mind to the Holy Spirit as you read this text.

The Spirit is the teacher of all truth, the One Who is fully aware of your pain and disappointment. I pray that somehow through the words on these pages, you will discover the Father's heart and find your place in His house. I pray that you will find healing and restoration in the broken places in your life.

Something gets broken inside a son the moment his father walks out. Some sacred thing. Some foundation. Some burning hope for all that only a father can offer a son - for guidance, for leadership, for an understanding of manhood and of brotherhood, for sonship, for belonging - for a name. Though he may not have the words to name it yet, he knows there is a gap in his identity. The boy is left holding these broken shards of what should have been a whole and firm foundation, and they often will not let him rest at night, though he has said his prayers. Though his mom has tucked him in, and the nightlight glows soft in the corner and all appears to be safe, this broken child lies awake, tears in his searching eyes, wondering if he'll ever be strong enough, tough enough, good enough - wondering why – why would his father have left him?

Does his father think of him now? Does he wonder how he is, what he needs? Who will show him how to shave? Who will teach him about girls? About love? And home? Who will fish with him, hunt with him, laugh with him, teach him to work? How will he grow into a man? The boy holds his hand toward the nightlight, watches its shadowy movement in the dark of the bedroom and wonders about his father's hands. All of the unknowns of manhood lurk in the shadowy hope of the future, and he longs to rest, secure in the knowledge that his dad will be there, will love him, will have the answers or find them, somehow, and in this fantasy, the boy will not be so broken, will not feel the burden of having to find these answers on his own.

Perhaps it was this early brokenness in me that helped to shape the very distorted view of God I developed growing up as an adopted child in a strict and legalistic church. Perhaps the fading image of the father who would slip away like a vapor in the night, seemingly never to think of me again, tainted this idea of God as Father – as a loving, merciful Father who sent His only Son to die for me. I was told that if I would repent and believe, He would forgive me and someday in the *sweet by-and-by*, I could go to heaven and live there with Him forever.

In the beginning, it sounded wonderful. What sensible person would refuse that offer; heaven or hell? Father or fatherlessness? Sonship or an orphan's life? Just that easy - just accept His Son and live; I was all in.

It wasn't until later that the image became tainted, distorted. I came to see God as an unpleasable and unfair ruler or dictator who, like my father, was somewhere out there, always somewhere out of reach – who had left me with the burden of expectation, afraid and flawed and on my own to figure it all out. There seemed to be no way to ever live up to the demands I thought He required of me. And then, for a short time, I went from being all-in to being all-out. Looking back, I can see it all more clearly. Though I wasn't aware of it at the time, I was absolutely biblically illiterate; I simply believed whatever the man in the pulpit preached or what the Sunday school teacher taught. That was not their fault; it was my responsibility to search for and to discover the truth. I was much like the children of Israel who said to Moses, "You speak to us and we will hear, but let not God speak to us lest we die!" **(Exodus 20:19)**.

Even today, many in the church take this approach, trusting another man with disseminating the truth, rather than seeking, searching, discerning for ourselves. The truth is that God had already said to Moses that what He wanted was a *kingdom of priests* **(Exodus 19:6)**. God's original plan was not a mediator system, but a *kingdom of sons*. God's plan for that despondent child, lying in the darkness, wondering, longing, yearning for a father who had chosen to leave was not some substitute, go-between father figure. His plan all along was sonship.

When I was sixteen years old, something pivotal happened in my life. It happened during a revival meeting that lasted for weeks. As the visiting evangelist stood at the front of the church, preparing to close the final meeting, he asked if anyone had a last request before he departed. I went forward and stood before him, wordless. I can't imagine what he expected when he looked at me and asked a simple question, "What do you want?"

Before I could process the question, the words flooded out of my mouth, "I want to know the truth." The words surprised even me. I had not been aware that I did not know the truth, that I was seeking or that I needed to seek any brand of truth. But in that moment, my spirit knew what my mind had not discerned. In that revival, I was introduced to the power of the Holy Spirit, and I was filled in a way that marked my life forever. And that one request has turned out to be quite possibly the most powerful prayer of my life. Unfortunately, standing there as a sixteen-year-old boy, I wasn't aware of all of that. I was very naïve and dysfunctional myself and I had no healthy pattern in my life to help me envision what a true Father – Son relationship looked like. I would open my religious prayers with the common term *Father*, but I made no conscious connection that I had lived my whole life, both naturally and spiritually, as an orphan. I may have been in the house, but I never knew the security and acceptance of being a true son. I always felt the need to perform and to seek affirmation in my efforts.

I didn't know until I was around ten years old that my natural father had walked out on my mother, my older sister and me when I was still an infant. When I was about three years old, I stood before a judge in Chattooga County Georgia and went through the adoption process with my mother's new husband. I have snapshot-memories of two moments on that day. They are etched in my memory - no words, no emotions, no sounds - just two still-life images hanging on the wall of my memory. One is of a giant clock, perched at the top of the building like the star at the top of a Christmas tree. The other is of the judge during the process. In both snapshots, I am aware of my place. In the first, I am on the steps ascending with the clock between me and the distant sky, and in the second, I am standing a few feet away from the judge on his bench. It strikes me now that in both memories my focus is on what is above me - the towering clock and the judge on his elevated bench. I, in juxtaposition, am beneath, and both the clock and the judge signify things that are completely out of my control.

In truth, I have very few memories of anything that happened in my life before about the age of ten. This is evidence that there is more to be uncovered. In hindsight, I can see that I moved quietly into denial, burying any notion of vulnerability, and I told myself that I didn't let it bother me most of my life. And for many years, I believed me.

The orphan heart is closed and defensive. It not only seeks to protect and hide from the dangers of the world, it also will hide vulnerability even from itself. Later, I would discover that most of my ambition and drive to succeed were born out of a rebellious spirit in order to prove that I could make it on my own. That same delusion I had about the Father-Son relationship carried right over into my spiritual walk.

But God brings us into light slowly, allowing our spiritual eyes to adjust and be prepared for more and more, and so it was many years later, even after being in pastoral ministry and having natural and spiritual sons and daughters, that a shift began to happen in my life. My wife and I had been in ministry for a long time and had been witnesses to the power of God. We had played active parts in a ministry in which numerous lives were saved, healed, and restored. I had also been in a relationship with spiritual fathers and had served some of them with my whole heart. I was no longer ignorant of the biblical pattern of sonship, but God was calling me deeper. This call to a Father–Son relationship was developing into something I had seemed to be missing. Was it possible that I was still living out of a wounded, orphaned heart? I was a senior leader, a pastor, a bishop! I was supposed to have it together. What was it that God was after? Just like He had taken me down the road of repentance and paradigm shifts in the past, I was being called deeper again even at this stage in my ministry. I was being called to re-examine the truth I already thought I understood, to look deeper - to press in.

And in this calling, I was reminded of my younger self. Vulnerable. Innocent. Longing for some truth so great that my spirit cried out for it. I meditated on that moment - when, somehow, my spirit knew and asked for the one thing I needed most, "I want the truth." The request became a resounding prayer that would echo over and over throughout my life and mark my course, as a Christian, as a believer, and as a minister of the gospel. Over and over through almost forty years, I have heard the Father's voice many times, reminding me of that request, nudging me toward the discomfort of truths that contradicted what I had always accepted without question, calling me to seek, to learn to observe all that He was showing me, and nudging me to humble myself as He taught me – as He continues to teach me. He was instructing me, as a good Father would.

You see, what Adam lost in the garden above all else was his relationship as a son with his Father. What Jesus, the last Adam came to restore, was that relationship. With that restoration comes all the benefits of being kingdom citizens, of being kings and priests as God originally designed. I am always mindful that God desired communion and not religious duties from Adam. Even in Adam's shame and fear, God came walking and talking – seeking what was lost – His connection with His son.

This writing is not an exhaustive study of the Father or the Son. It is one man's journey to the Father's house in faith that he is ever evolving into a confident and secure son – a son who, even in the process of this evolution, can say with full confidence that he knows who and whose he is. It is a call for all of us to discover our true identities as sons and to heed the call to maturity, the call to understand the household of faith and how we properly relate to our spiritual leaders and one another. It is very simply an invitation to come home.

CHAPTER TWO

A Fatherless Generation

*For although you could have countless babysitters in
Christ telling you what you're doing wrong, you don't
have many fathers who correct you in love. But I'm a
true father to you, for I became your father when I gave
you the gospel and brought you into union with Jesus, the
Anointed One. So I encourage you, my children, to follow
the example that I live before you.*
(1 Corinthians 4:15-16, TPT)

We experience many different levels of influence from teachers,
coaches, mentors and instructors in our lives. Most of my
teachers were good teachers. They did what they were contracted
to do; they taught me the alphabet, proper punctuation,
mathematical concepts and practices, even logical reasoning and
civic responsibility. My education has served me well, and I am
grateful. I needed those teachers. But once in a while, a teacher
will step past his or her contracted role and into a spiritual role
with a student. Once in a while, a teacher becomes more than a
teacher. I had two teachers who saw that I needed fathering and
stepped into what I now recognize as a father's role.

The first was a coach who mentored me beyond academics or

sports. Coach Daniels was my seventh-grade teacher and my football coach throughout junior high and high school. He is the first teacher I remember really connecting with me in a personal way. He invested in my thinking, planting ideas, ideals, structures, supports, and even questions that prodded me to seek a greater truth about my future and my own investment in that future than I had considered before. I will always be grateful for his mentorship. He gave me a different kind of perspective on what it was to be a man.

And then there was Mr. Dawson. Mr. Dawson was my electronics teacher. I attended a small high school in rural Alabama, which meant the school was limited in the offerings for electives, but we could sign up to attend an off-campus technical school that served students from different schools throughout the county. Students could be bussed there, or we could drive. I had been working since I was fourteen years old, and I'd acquired a car that would just barely get me there. Looking back, I can see that it wasn't even safe to drive, actually, but as a young boy, none of that bothered me. I had wheels!

I had an interest in electronics and decided I wanted to give tech school a try. Having worked for a few years already, I had an idea of what it was about, and I had decided that the best plan for me was to join the military. In fact, I had pre-joined, but I wound up having a football injury that took my knee out. After that, I was unable to pass the physical.

When Mr. Dawson found out about this, he asked me, "What are you going to do?" I was speechless. The military had been my best idea. My work ethic was strong, but opportunities for someone like me with limited means and perhaps even more limited support from home were not abundant. "Why don't you at least consider technical college?" he asked. I was dumbfounded. This was a thought I would never have had on my own. How could I? College was expensive and time-consuming. How could I pay for it if I didn't work, and how could I work enough to pay for it and still have time to study and go to class? Perhaps even more daunting, how would I have money on which to live? Mr. Dawson's hand fell reassuringly on my shoulder. "It will work out," he told me. And he was right.

One day before the end of the semester, Mr. Dawson sent me to see the school counselor. When I sat down in his office, the counselor informed me that I had received a full scholarship to Alabama Technical College. I could not have been more surprised at this news. You see, I had never applied for a scholarship. Mr. Dawson had applied for me. Now that the question of college was answered, Mr. Dawson had one more plan for me. "How do you plan to get to college, son?" he asked me one day.

"I'll figure it out," I answered, knowing full well that the car I was driving was unsafe at best and would not get me there for the first trip, let alone any kind of travel back and forth.

Apparently Mr. Dawson knew that, too. "Let's go to the bank," he instructed, and I followed him to his car. Inside the bank, Mr. Dawson spoke to someone he obviously knew. "This boy needs three-thousand dollars," he said. Papers were signed, hands were shaken, and I somehow walked out with enough money to buy a decent used car that would last me throughout my college career.

"It will work out," Mr. Dawson had assured me. And then, he had stepped out beyond all reasonable expectations and worked it out, himself. Clearly, he saw something in me that I had never had the opportunity to see before. His investment in my life is one that continues to yield returns, and even now, recounting this story can bring tears to my eyes. This was one of my first glimpses of what father-love can look like, and it came from a man who had no blood or familial investment in my life.

I am grateful for every teacher I ever had. I am grateful for all that I learned and all the questions that were born in me that make me the thinker I am today. But those two men stand apart. Coach Daniels invested in my worth, my value. He was the first person who ever talked to me like a man. As for Mr. Dawson, this man stepped beyond mentor and into the realm of fatherly provision. I don't know how he knew to do the things my father should have been doing. I don't know why he took the risk. I don't know if he crossed any ethical lines in signing that loan for me, but I do know he changed the trajectory of my life. I don't know what my life would be right now had he not invested in me.

At the core of my being, I know that these men who poured their wisdom, time and support into my life were not just doing it out of a responsibility to a contract. They were not explicitly instructing me in those moments, though I was learning so much. They were fathering me. They were filling in gaps that were clearly obvious to them. And in so doing, they gave me a glimpse - an inkling that would later open windows to greater understanding - of what it meant to be fathered.

I know that I was just one of so many young men, moving toward adulthood without a loving, nurturing father as a guide. Just one of so many who so much needed that glimpse. I am astounded by the grace afforded me in the actions of these two amazing men.

Fatherhood is a multi-faceted role - a role into which multiple roles are woven. No doubt, the man who married my mother and climbed the courthouse steps with my sister and me to legally adopt us, the man who stood before the judge that day and promised to father us, had strong ideas about what that fathering would mean. I have to say that many of those roles were fulfilled. He provided for us. He stayed with my mother and with the family. He corrected us. He was what my biological father was not; he was there. But true fatherhood embodies spiritual aspects: connection, investment, teaching - pressure, yes, but also support to match that pressure. True fatherhood builds faith and guides a son to find the lighted path of his own future. Fatherhood is a spiritual matter, and without a father, the lack of identity encapsulated in an orphan heart will constantly haunt, limit and likely keep us in the same dysfunctional cycles handed down from one generation to the other.

This inherited dysfunction keeps the cycle going from one generation to another. We see it in the home and in the church.

So many of our sons are hiding in shame and guilt because of dysfunctional father – son relationships. We often expect our sons to grow up into maturity and responsibility before we establish a heart of freedom, healing and worth. The affirmation of a father's voice is a spiritual dynamic. If you ever lived without it and later experienced it, you know it is life-changing. It is like water on a dry and thirsty land. It does not operate at the mind level; it penetrates the heart.

So even in a home in which the father met that minimum bar -just staying - even then, a child can feel, and in a practical sense, actually be without the guidance and support of a father. The orphan's heart feels abandoned, isolated and lonely, even if a father is in the house. What is missing is much deeper than a place to sleep, food to eat, and clothes to wear. For someone like me, abandoned by my biological father and kept at arm's-length by my adopted father, it can impact our ideas about what fatherhood is, about who we are and about what our worth is in this life. It can make us feel utterly alone. The orphan heart desperately needs the affirmation that only comes from the unconditionally accepting embrace of a father.

This affirmation of the Father can come from multiple people who come into our lives over time. Remember, it is a spiritual matter. Perhaps that is the greatest lesson Coach Daniels and Mr. Dawson taught me. All we have to do is look around at the state of so many languishing in our current society, and there is no doubt what our world becomes in the absence of true fathers in our homes. There are so many books, documented studies, and statistics readily available to support this claim: the collapse of our moral society (specifically the family unit) is largely a result of men failing to fulfill our God-given roles as fathers.

There were more examples of fatherly connection that I noticed as a young man. Even today, they are highlighted in my spirit. These moments are important - are powerful. At the time, I didn't fully understand them, but I knew enough to pay attention - to allow God to write them on my heart. One in particular I have not mentioned yet, perhaps because it is a more painful example than the ones I've relayed above. It is the example my adopted father - the one I call Dad - showed me in his interactions with my brother, who was actually his biological son. I would have had to have been blind not to see it - the way he spoke to my brother, the way they interacted, the understanding automatically given out of love. I witnessed beautiful, fatherly moments with many of my friends and their fathers, and I now believe that was one of the reasons I wanted to be at their houses, to spend time with them on the football field, to see how their fathers encouraged them before and after the games and supported them even in their practice.

I remember seeing that and feeling the warmth, feeling an incredible amount of respect and inspiration from it. However, there was a stark difference in the way I felt when I witnessed my brother receiving those same types of encouragement and support from the man I, too, called dad. I was seven years older than my brother. He was a kid to me. I don't remember feeling jealousy or resentment toward him or my dad in any way. I just remember noticing. Witnessing those moments made me feel more alone, less respected, less loved, and, most tragic of all, less worthy. They made me feel as if I were being abandoned - not just again, but over and over again.

C.S.Lewis said, "A man does not call a line crooked unless he has some idea of what is a straight line" (**Lewis, p**).

I am grateful for these glimpses, because they helped me understand, at the very least, what I was missing. And that understanding was a fertile seed in what grew to be my decision to embrace fatherhood full-force, however falteringly and in what eventually led me to embrace the God of all hope as a good and loving father. Some people learn the love of a father through the continual pouring of affection and attention - of connection. I'm not talking about perfection; none of us can claim that, but of intention and affection and the commitment to be there emotionally and physically and in any other way a child might need. Some people learn that through living it. Others, like me, learn it by peering at it, as if through a window, watching others receive. It brings to mind the image of Hans Christian Andersen's little match girl, peering through the window at the glow of a hearth whose warmth could have saved her. It is sad, but it isn't the saddest scenario. There are still others who never see evidence of a father's love, and so they never have that seed planted. They live their lives as fathers the same way their fathers led theirs, because they don't have a vision for any other life. And so the cycle continues.

Not long ago, as I first began to meditate and to consider writing this text, there was yet another tragic mass shooting in our nation. All of the usual anti-gun and pro-second amendment folks took to their corners. The debates raged for a short time, but they eventually subsided, and we were back to normal - business as usual.

In the aftermath of the shooting, I sat listening to one of the talking heads on the news, and he said something like this, "It is clear that we can't all agree on all these controversial political issues, but I know we all can agree that this man deserves to be in hell."

In that moment, a holy anger and a heart-wrenching cry came from my inner being, and I felt the fire of righteous indignation such as I have felt few times in my life. In that fiery moment I heard, as if I were hearing someone else respond, two short but powerful words, roaring out of my being, "Hell, No!" I didn't agree, and I still don't agree. We cannot all agree on that. This young man was once a precious baby, fresh from the womb, handed to a mother. A baby with a life force and potential and needs that would not be met. And while I do not wish this to be interpreted as an excuse for the young man, I fear that we can all too easily take the secular view of good versus evil, rallying for this idea of evil people - the villains, if you will - finally getting the hell they deserve while the rest of us ride the waves of grace into heaven. Because we are good, right? Heaven help us if we fall into the pattern of thinking that leads us to be glad anyone - any precious soul created in the image and likeness of God - might be burning in hell.

At the time I heard the commentator's assertion, I had been praying already, like many believers, for the nation and for first responders and victims when the thought of the shooter hit me. We quickly wanted to know all about him:

What's his name?
What is on his Facebook and other social media pages?

Is he a racist?

Is he a homophobe?

Is he a nationalist, a socialist, a Republican or a Democrat?

Was this a hate crime or an act of political terrorism?

As soon as I saw a picture of the shooter and the breaking news gave the nation his name, I heard a different set of questions in my spirit - questions I didn't hear anyone else asking:

- *Where was his father?*
- *Whose son is he?*
- *To whom did he belong?*
- *Who and what created such anger and rage in this young man to blind him of the value and dignity of every human being?*

This tragedy was not the first of its kind in our nation. We've seen this horror show before. But, as I happened to be focused on gathering data and statistics for this writing at the time, I spent some time reviewing the history of mass shootings in the US. I was stunned that the shooter in almost every instance was a young man who had suffered the loss of his identity and had no father in his life to affirm, nurture and protect him. Again, I am not excusing the actions of anyone, but make no mistake about it; these angry young men who are filled with hatred are broken, and we as a society, and especially as Christians, must step up and answer their cries before the next horror show comes to our town.

The truth that we often don't want to see is that, whenever

there is an extreme level of abuse, you will likely see an extreme reaction or overreaction. As a man, I know that it is impossible for me to fully comprehend the pain and suffering of being treated with the bias or prejudice that many women have faced in our culture through the ages. However, I can relate to receiving unfair treatment as second class or inferior for other reasons. In my case, my first reaction was generally to retaliate and try to prove them wrong. In fact, part of my maturing as a son involved coming to grips with the truth that much of my drive for success was an extreme reaction to feeling neglected and unappreciated. In this way, good came from the struggle. This attitude helped me to survive, but it did not serve me well, because in this way of operating, we don't trust people. In the kingdom of God, we are called to a vulnerability that requires that we trust more than ourselves - that we trust God and people. That level of trust is necessary if we are to heal by making choices that don't cause different issues along the way.

Some people have become so extreme in their support of women's rights and equal opportunity, it seems that they feel it is necessary to diminish and even punish men for being male, even more so if they are dealing with a white male. It is human nature to feel better about punishing someone for a problem rather than going deep to the root to identify the origin of the problem. It is not necessary to diminish one gender or race in order to elevate the other. This becomes another side to the same dysfunctional and fear-based coin. We can only see the full expression of the Father's nature and heart when both men and women of all ethnicities are recognized as both equal and beautifully unique parts of His divine nature.

The pendulum has to be steadied by a loving and caring hand, or it will just continue to swing violently from one extreme to the other. There must be peacemakers and bridge-builders if we will ever know real and lasting equality, justice, and unity. There must be someone willing to be in the center, reaching out to all sides. It is much easier to take sides than it is to stand in the gap or in the center. Often, taking this position - this belief that we don't have to hate one to love the other - leaves us at odds with both camps. It is as if loving one diminishes the love for the other, and that, of course, is not how the love of God works. Bridges are both costly and time-consuming, and while they may be appreciated greatly "bye and bye", a bridge under construction is difficult to trust in and, quite often, feels like a nuisance. It gets in the way of our comfort zones.

Much of the crisis of our society can easily be traced to the deterioration of the family unit. The dysfunctional family is now the new normal in our society, and one could argue that the statistics are not much, if any, better in the church.

> *The most important domestic challenge facing the U.S. at the close of the twentieth century is the re-creation of fatherhood as a vital social role for men. At stake is nothing less than the success of the American experiment. For unless we reverse the trend of fatherlessness, no other set of accomplishments--not economic growth nor prison construction nor welfare reform nor better schools—will succeed in arresting the decline of child well-being and the spread of male violence. To tolerate the trend of fatherlessness is to accept the inevitability of continued social recession.*
> -David Blankenhorn: Fatherless America.

According to the 2020 U.S. Census 18.4 million children are living without a biological father. This means that out of the 73 million children in the U.S. 23% are without a present father.

https://thefatherlessgeneration.wordpress.com/statistics/

- 63% of youth suicides are from fatherless homes (US Dept. Of Health/Census) – 5 times the average.
- 90% of all homeless and runaway children are from fatherless homes – 32 times the average.
- 85% of all children who show behavior disorders come from fatherless homes – 20 times the average. (Center for Disease Control)
- 80% of rapists with anger problems come from fatherless homes –14 times the average. (Justice & Behavior, Vol 14, 403-426)
- 71% of all high school dropouts come from fatherless homes – 9 times the average. (National Principals Association Report)

Father Factor in Education – Fatherless children are twice as likely to drop out of school.

- Children with Fathers who are involved are 40% less likely to repeat a grade in school.
- Children with Fathers who are involved are 70% less likely to drop out of school.
- Children with Fathers who are involved are more likely to get A's in school.
- Children with Fathers who are involved are more likely

to enjoy school and engage in extracurricular activities.

- 75% of all adolescent patients in chemical abuse centers come from fatherless homes – 10 times higher than the average.

Father Factor in Drug and Alcohol Abuse – Researchers at Columbia University found that children living in two-parent households with a poor relationship with their father are 68% more likely to smoke, drink, or use drugs compared to all teens in two-parent households. Teens in single mother households are at a 30% higher risk than those in two-parent households.

- 70% of youths in state-operated institutions come from fatherless homes – 9 times the average. (U.S. Dept. of Justice, Sept. 1988)
- 85% of all youths in prison come from fatherless homes – 20 times the average. (Fulton Co. Georgia, Texas Dept. of Correction)

Father Factor in Incarceration – Even after controlling for income, youths in father-absent households still had significantly higher odds of incarceration than those in mother -father families. Youths who never had a father in the household experienced the highest odds. A 2002 Department of Justice survey of 7,000 inmates revealed that 39% of jail inmates lived in mother-only households. Approximately forty-six percent of jail inmates in 2002 had a previously incarcerated family member. One-fifth experienced a father in prison or jail.

Father Factor in Crime – A study of 109 juvenile offenders indicated that family structure significantly contributes to personal delinquencies. Adolescents, particularly boys, in single-parent families were at higher risk of status, property and personal delinquencies. Moreover, students attending schools with a high proportion of children of single parents are also at risk. A study of 13,986 women in prison showed that more than half grew up without their father. Forty-two percent grew up in a single-mother household and sixteen percent lived with neither parent

Father Factor in Child Abuse – Compared to living with both parents, living in a single-parent home doubles the risk that a child will suffer physical, emotional, or educational neglect. The overall rate of child abuse and neglect in single-parent households is 27.3 children per 1,000, whereas the rate of overall maltreatment in two-parent households is 15.5 per 1,000.

Daughters of single parents without a Father involved are 53% more likely to marry as teenagers, 71% more likely to have children as teenagers, 164% more likely to have a pre-marital birth and 92% more likely to get divorced themselves.

Adolescent girls raised in a 2 parent home with involved Fathers are significantly less likely to be sexually active than girls raised without involved Fathers.

- 43% of US children live without their father [US Department of Census]
- 90% of homeless and runaway children are from fatherless homes. [US D.H.H.S., Bureau of the Census]
- 80% of rapists motivated with displaced anger come

from fatherless homes. [Criminal Justice & Behaviour, Vol 14, pp. 403-26, 1978]

- 71% of pregnant teenagers lack a father.
  [U.S. Department of Health and Human Services press release, Friday, March 26, 1999]
- 63% of youth suicides are from fatherless homes.
  [US D.H.H.S., Bureau of the Census]
- 85% of children who exhibit behavioral disorders come from fatherless homes. [Center for Disease Control]
- 90% of adolescent repeat arsonists live with only their mother. [Wray Herbert, "Dousing the Kindlers," Psychology Today, January, 1985, p. 28]
- 71% of high school dropouts come from fatherless homes. [National Principals Association Report on the State of High Schools]
- 75% of adolescent patients in chemical abuse centers come from fatherless homes. [Rainbows for all God's Children]
- 70% of juveniles in state operated institutions have no father. [US Department of Justice, Special Report, Sept. 1988]
- 85% of youths in prisons grew up in a fatherless home. [Fulton County Georgia jail populations, Texas Department of Corrections, 1992]

Fatherless boys and girls are: twice as likely to drop out of high school, twice as likely to end up in jail, and four times more likely to need help for emotional or behavioral problems. [US D.H.H.S. news release, March 26, 1999]

Census Fatherhood Statistics
- 64.3 million: Estimated number of fathers across the nation
- 26.5 million: Number of fathers who are part of married-couple families with their own children under the age of 18.

Among these fathers –
- 22 percent are raising three or more of their own children under 18 years old (among married-couple family households only).
- 2 percent live in the home of a relative or a non-relative.
- 2.5 million: Number of single fathers, up from 400,000 in 1970. Currently, among single parents living with their children, 18 percent are men.

Among these fathers –
- 8 percent are raising three or more of their own children under 18 years old.
- 42 percent are divorced, 38 percent have never married, 16 percent are separated and 4 percent are widowed. (The percentages of those divorced and never married are not significantly different from one another.)
- 16 percent live in the home of a relative or a non-relative.
- 27 percent have an annual family income of $50,000 or more.
- 85 percent: Among the 30.2 million fathers living with children younger than 18, the percentage who lived with their biological children only.
- 11 percent lived with step-children
- 4 percent with adopted children
- < 1 percent with foster children

Of course, we know this. We know this. It's rare to watch a movie that depicts men who are caught up in a cycle of preying on vulnerable women without hearing at least one crass joke about daddy issues. We know this. The father-absence crisis in America is clear. We exist in a fatherless generation. And what are we doing about it? In many cases, we have devolved into just deciding that it isn't important at all. Many people believe that family structure doesn't really matter, as long as children are cared for and loved by someone, anyone. Perhaps we are settling. Perhaps it's a compromise we've embraced because there is no easier fix for the crisis we face. I can't speak definitively on that - I can only draw my conclusions based on biblical patterns, principles and personal experience.

Can a child be raised by a single mother? Can a child be raised in an orphanage or foster-care home? Can an adopted child get the same nurture and love as any other? These are complex questions with no simple answers. My answer is, possibly. Can you slice bread with an ax? Can a surgeon operate with a swiss army knife? There are too many complex questions to just spout off generic answers with cookie cutter language and stale statistics. But we can know that there are better answers and better methods if we look humbly and honestly at the problems while avoiding looking for someone to blame.

Perhaps the better questions are these: How did God create us, and what are His best plans? It is clear that there is a difference in a mother's approach to raising a child compared to that of a father. We cannot dismiss that we can be equal and yet vastly different in so many areas. This may be the best indication that we benefit most from having both, rather than clinging to a "which one is the best" approach. Raising a child is not a competition; it's a partnership.

I must say again that this is not simply the gender factor, but more of a spiritual matter. It is also clear that having a male and female parenting situation does not automatically guarantee a healthy environment for child development.

I personally grew up in a mother and step-father home, but I have to be honest and say that the nurturing, affirmation and discipline was a bit dysfunctional. I certainly contributed to the problem with my orphan heart and the resentment and perpetual disappointment I held based on what I was not receiving blinded me to my own shortcomings.

> *"According to sociobiology, genetic preservation is at the core of human behavior. Because it is inherent in our genetic structure to ensure survival, individuals are predisposed to take measures to guarantee their genetic survival. In other words, they favor strategies and methods that will increase the likelihood of their family lineage being carried on. Based on these theories, it could be assumed that stepchildren are more likely to be abused by parents than biological children. In fact, some research has provided evidence of a 5-fold increase in risk of child abuse for step-children compared to biological children. There is abundant evidence that children living in stepfamilies are more likely to experience sexual abuse."* **(Good Therapy)**

While the following statistics are formidable, the Responsible Fatherhood research literature generally supports the claim that a loving and nurturing father improves outcomes for children, families and communities.

- Children with involved, loving fathers are significantly more likely to do well in school, have healthy self-esteem, exhibit empathy and prosocial behavior, and avoid high-risk behaviors such as drug use, truancy, and criminal activity compared to children who have uninvolved fathers.
- Studies on parent-child relationships and child wellbeing show that father love is an important factor in predicting the social, emotional, and cognitive development and functioning of children and young adults.
- 43 percent of first marriages dissolve within fifteen years, about 60 percent of divorcing couples have children, and approximately one million children each year experience the divorce of their parents.
- Compared to children born within marriage, children born to cohabiting parents are three times as likely to experience father absence, and children born to unmarried, non-cohabiting parents are four times as likely to live in a father-absent home.
- About 40 percent of children in father-absent homes have not seen their father at all during the past year, 26 percent of absent fathers live in a different state than their children, and 50 percent of children living absent their father have never set foot in their father's home.
- Children who live absent their biological fathers are,

on average, at least two to three times more likely to be poor, to use drugs, to experience educational, health, emotional and behavioral problems, to be victims of child abuse, and to engage in criminal behavior than their peers who live with their married, biological (or adoptive) parents.

In the absence of real answers – in the absence of Truth – many children, especially as they form ideals during adolescence - will eventually seek out counterfeit values to ease the nagging questions about who they are and why they exist. These children are already statistics, though they quite frequently feel frightfully alone. They have fallen into this situation through no fault of their own, and while they may not be aware of how many others are dealing with the same struggles, neither are they blind to the brokenness that comes from being left behind. And we fall into this cycle that somehow keeps us accepting the status quo with a frightening level of complacency. We see the news and read the statistics. We even see children who are living numbers feeding those statistics all around us. But what is the answer? Can we pass laws or create new social welfare programs and turn the tide? Is it possible that the Father of all creation has already given us answers that we need to rediscover?

I propose that we can rediscover the ancient plans and find healing for our land, especially for our families. God has given us access to his thoughts and divine wisdom. We cannot rely on human wisdom and intellect to solve such matters of the spirit and heart.

True spirituality that is pure in the eyes of our Father God is to make a difference in the lives of the orphans, and widows in their troubles, and to refuse to be corrupted by the world's values.
(James 1:27, TPT)

CHAPTER THREE

Turning Our Hearts

Look, I am sending you the prophet Elijah before the great and dreadful day of the LORD arrives. His preaching will turn the hearts of fathers to their children, and the hearts of children to their fathers. Otherwise I will come and strike the land with a curse. (**Malachi 4:5-6, NLT**)

First and last things are weighty – extremely important. As the writing of the Old Testament comes to a close, we have this prophetic promise. The day will come when something so profound will happen that it will impact all the earth with a blessing or curse! That prophetic promise is connected to two things. First, the hearts of fathers will turn. This indicates that the initial step has to do with the posture of the father's heart. In my case and many others, I have seen that this initial step is a difficult process if we are peering out at life from the windows of an orphaned heart. It is easier to pretend everything is okay, easier not to look at the hard facts, easier not to try to make amends when we have no idea whether amends can be made, and when, in fact, we have no idea how to be vulnerable. The modeling of all of that is required of the father. The father is the first cog in the wheel, and when we are vulnerable enough to let our hearts turn, then secondly, the hearts of the children will turn. For the orphaned heart, the vulnerability to take this step is deep and frightening, for whose model do we have? Where is the example we can trust? On whose shoulders will we stand?

I find it interesting that this insight from the book of Malachi shows that the fathers' hearts must turn first, and the children's hearts will follow suit. It points to cause and effect. It implies a sort of modeling on the part of the father that impacts and changes the child. Interestingly, it is Elijah whom God sends to preach the Word to these men. Elijah is the only prophet in the Old Testament who is recorded as having had a protege - a mentee - a son-figure, if you will, Elisha. None of the other prophets show a record of mentoring a successor, not until Jesus arrives in the New Testament do we see this kind of mentoring again.

Before Elijah was caught in the whirlwind, he asked Elisha what he wanted. He answered that he wanted a double portion of what Elijah had. The double portion, of course, is the first-born inheritance. Elisha was asking for and claiming sonship. And when Elijah ascended, Elisha called out, *"My father, my father!"* (**2 Kings 2:9-12**)

So Elijah, of course, is the perfect prophet to preach this important and powerful word. He knows what it is to connect with one who is following his lead. He knows the power of this connection and the importance of it. He knows the responsibility too. He knows that the difference between blessing and cursing, between connection and abandonment, is not in the hands of the children, nor is it in the hands of the prophet, himself. The difference is in the hearts of the fathers. In the position of these hearts that should (if we can reason what should be in a rational sense) naturally turn toward their sons and the willingness of these fathers to put egos aside and turn their hearts toward their children.

This thought of the heart turning is intriguing. It implies that the heart is capable of looking or leaning in a certain direction. Could it be that our hearts can see, as if they have eyes? Can our hearts be - by choice or even subconsciously - turned toward or away from someone or something? Can our hearts be distracted, like our vision? Could the vision of our hearts be blurred or veiled?

As I pondered this, I had this image of sitting at an intersection, and this homeless person was sitting there with a sign. In such a moment, we make a choice. Do we reach out the window with a dollar or two (or more)? Sometimes, especially if we don't have cash or if it is not readily available, we don't lower the window. Sometimes we intentionally avoid eye contact, willing ourselves to look at the light or the street sign or the person in the passenger seat. It's an uncomfortable few moments. We consciously and intentionally don't look sometimes, as if our not seeing would make him less hungry or us less responsible - as if we could choose not to see and somehow be exonerated when Jesus says, "I was hungry and you fed me not." The truth of it struck me - how we adjust what we are willing to see when we don't have the resources or the time or the will to give to someone whose presence requires it of us.

In the same way, if the heart is sick or wounded, it will greatly influence how we posture ourselves in every relationship. It is possible to be present physically and for the heart to be completely disconnected or - perhaps even worse - to consciously choose to look the other way.

Consider the various heart-centered metaphors we employ in normal, everyday conversation. One has a broken heart, his heart is stirred, he is faint of heart, his heart melts or hardens, grows smitten or gets stolen. Her heart is glad or pure, merry or wise. Perhaps she has a willing heart or is consistently kind-hearted. The existence of these metaphors in our current culture conveys the importance of a heart-level choice. It goes beyond changing one's mind; a heart issue is an issue of depth, and to turn one's heart toward or away from anything implies a spiritual, core decision - a life-altering turn.

In his book, *Simplicity: The Freedom of Letting Go*, Richard Rohr recounts an enlightening experience he had while visiting a family. At some point during their visit, the youngest of the three boys was running through the house and fell down the stairs. Following the fall, there was a frightening silence, alarming the adults who had been about their conversations in a different room. Alarmed, they all ran to the child to check on him, to find his eyes open as he lay silent and still. Rorh finishes the story this way:

> *Christopher lay at the foot of the stairs. And his big brown eyes looked up inquiringly at his father, as if to say, "Did I hurt myself?" His father ran down to him, took him in his*

arms, and the *instant his father's arms enfolded him, the boy began to scream and cry. I wondered why this little boy needed seven seconds before he felt pain, but at the same moment the answer occurred to me…the little boy couldn't feel and admit the pain until he was sufficiently sure that love was there.* (**Rohr, 146**)

Vulnerability demands felt-safety. It is only when we are safe and whole that we can be vulnerable enough to give our hearts to any relationship. Even the best Father ever, God himself, desires one thing – that we love Him with our whole hearts. We can only fully love this way when our hearts are free from fear, shame, and insecurity. It requires that we forgive ourselves and allow God's forgiveness to do its perfect work in us. That we trust. That we, like Christopher, trust the Father enough to look up into his eyes, let go of whatever is holding us back from acknowledging the pain or the fear or the shame we've stumbled into, and allow Him to take us into His arms. Loving God with our whole hearts demands vulnerability - that we move out of a place of self-protection and to acknowledge the presence of love and a faith that we are precious - truly precious - to Him. It requires that we turn, not just our minds, but our hearts toward him.

In the western world, we are programmed to analyze and reason through everything. In the modern church, we have a tendency to relate to God intellectually, with the head, but when God says, "Love me with all your heart," it bypasses intellectual thought or understanding. It goes deeper than that. Religion so many times gives us the intellectual approach to a heart matter.

We serve an intelligent Creator, who is also the embodiment of Love, itself. We are called to walk and to live in the truth of both our intellectual understanding and our open and vulnerable hearts.

God is not the author of confusion. He is always intentional and orderly, and we can be sure that He is full of wisdom in His purpose and plans. So, how important is it that He chose the order or pattern for restoration and reconciliation and that He connected all of redemption's hope to a Father – Son paradigm? He could have come with heaven's armies and conquered sin and darkness. However, He came in the form of a son, united so seamlessly with His Father that Jesus said, "If you have seen me, you have seen the Father."

My early hopes and expectations of salvation were very narrow and shallow: *Just give me a cabin in glory when I die.* Actually, I can see now that they were a little selfish. Eternal life in my mind was simply living forever on the other side, and especially avoiding eternal torment of hellfire and brimstone. I had my fire insurance and just hoped to hang on long enough to make it to the Promised land. I had no idea that eternal life was a quality of life we could have here and now. Jesus says in John 17:3, "Eternal life is to know God." I had no concept of God's big agenda, no idea that His vision has always been about being our Father. God never desired to be a landlord. His central goal was never about a place; it was about people – family!

Matthew 15:8 says, "These people love me with their lips, but their hearts are far from me." We love God through our own understanding of how to show Him love - with sermons and songs, with rituals, with words, and all of those things are valid parts of the Christian experience. However, He says, "Love me with your whole heart." Think about that. Your heart in its entirety. Ultimately, there is no logic in true faith; it is a heart walk. We build our lives on faith in an invisible God - one of the few consistent ideas throughout the Scriptures is the essence of this. "The just shall live by faith." **(Hebrews 10:38)**

The power of a father-son relationship exists in heart connection. We would be hard pressed to find a man who has a solid respect for the father he has never known. Knowing who our fathers are will never be enough. Living in the same home isn't even enough. The kind of healthy relationship a son needs requires a heart-level connection. It requires knowing and seeking to know one another. It involves supporting, respecting, correcting… loving. Additionally, in our walks with God, the Father, we need the same heart connection. In the church, how do we love God? We love him with sermons and songs, with rituals, but he says, "Love me with your whole heart." We seek to know him, but we must also commit to love him and to receive His love.

Even when Moses led the children of Israel out to the wilderness, God instructed Moses to build a tabernacle so that He could dwell among the people. In **Exodus 25:22** - God gave Moses the instructions for how to build the tabernacle and what to put in it. When he gave instructions for how to build the mercy seat, he put two cherubims on it, and he put them face to face. God said, "And I will commune with you there." This is a beautiful promise, and it embodies God's desire for us to have face-to-face union, not just with him, but with each other. The cherubims don't represent God; they represent us. When we are face to face, God is in the midst. Even under the old covenant, God desired to be with man on earth. Union has always been God's desire.

The core of His plan has always been family – not just family or families in general, His Family. When He said, "Let Us make man in Our image…", It is as if He was saying, "I want a family." He planned to have children to give His heritage to, and that desire has never changed. Before He conceived us, His heart was turned to us. The fact that the Father "sent His son" as a seed to be planted in the earth should give a hint of the harvest He was expecting. If He planted a son, what else could the harvest be except many sons? As His children, we are His offspring. We really are joint-heirs with Jesus – the Son of God. We have been united together in His Sonship.

We see a glimpse of the relationship He desired modeled in the beginning. We see the sweetness and communion that can only happen in a family united. God walking with us in the cool of the day. That is the relationship God created for us. That is who we really are. His relentless desire for us has never changed. His plan has always been to get us back to the garden, face-to-face, heart-to-heart.

Don't let your hearts be troubled. Trust in God, and trust also in me. There is more than enough room in my Father's home. If this were not so, would I have told you that I am going to prepare a place for you? **(John 14:1-2, NLT)**

When Jesus said that He was "going to prepare a place" for us, He never intended to go somewhere to start building a city, a mansion or a cabin. He was going to restore and reconcile what had been lost in the garden when Adam lost his Son-consciousness and became sin-conscious. Jesus *was going to the Father* so we could be *where He is* - not simply be where He is going geographically, but more importantly, to a place where we can be together. Where is He anyway? Later in the same chapter, Jesus added a profound promise. He said that He and the Father were going to take up residence in us. We are His "abode". We are His mansion. We are His garden. We are His temple. This is why we will never be condemned. He does not dwell in a condemned house.

Jesus replied, All who love me will do what I say. My Father will love them, and we will come and make our home with each of them. (**John 14:23, NLT**)

But Christ, as the Son, is in charge of God's entire house. And we are God's house, if we keep our courage and remain confident in our hope in Christ. (**Hebrews 3:6, NLT**)

Do you see this? The Son is in charge of God's house - not angels or demons – the Son.

Once I saw that God's original plan was for a family and specifically the Father – Son relationship, my heart began to turn. Now, so many of the scriptures relating to salvation became much more applicable, empowering, and liberating. Now that we have received him, we have been empowered and authorized officially to "become sons of God." Our identity is secure, but our maturity is part of the becoming process. It is a life-long journey of growth and increasing intimacy with our loving Father.

> *But as many as received him, to them gave he power*
> *to become the sons of God, even to them that believe*
> *on his name.* (John 1:12, KJV)

One of my favorite sayings is, "Enjoy the journey." I am learning to enjoy life in the present moment. Too often we miss the beauty of now because we are too focused on the next. I have five grandchildren from ages five to thirteen, and my own children are now in their thirties. I am thoroughly enjoying each of them in their present stages of life. I have a feeling that God is doing the same with each of His sons.

The mature children of God are those who are moved by the impulses of the Holy Spirit. We did not receive the "spirit of religious duty," leading us back into the fear of never being good enough. Instead, we have received the "Spirit of full acceptance," enfolding us into the family of God. We will never feel orphaned, for as He rises up within us, our spirits join Him in saying the words of tender affection, "Beloved Father!" For the Holy Spirit makes God's fatherhood real to us, whispering into our inner-most being, "You are God's beloved child!" Since we are His true children, we qualify to share all His treasures, for indeed, we are heirs of God himself, and since we are joined to Christ, we also inherit all that He is and all that He has. We will experience being co-glorified with Him, provided that we accept his sufferings as our own (Romans 8:14-17, TPT).

When we commit to this spiritual family, we do not just receive the Spirit; we receive the Spirit as His sons and daughters. The Holy Spirit moves us, and in so doing, convinces us of our righteousness and acceptance by the Father. We are no longer orphans, searching for a place to belong. We become convinced of His fatherhood. We are embraced and accepted. We are valued. We are chosen. This happens in our innermost being – the heart. His heart has always been turned to us, and now, we are free to turn our hearts to Him.

God did not just send us His spirit; He has put within us sonship! Listen for His voice within, affirming, *"You are my beloved son."* This is how the heart is turned. We turn from our religious duties of working and striving in order to be accepted to a place of receiving - by grace - His love and acceptance. When the heart turns, a veil is taken away, and we see Him clearly – we see ourselves as He sees us. We are now joined to Christ and are one with Him. There is no separation now that the hearts are turned toward one another. Now, we are qualified and justified in His sight. Now, we share in all His treasures! This is not some futuristic fantasy; this is available now!

God has brought me through so many seasons of repentance (changing my mind) over the years. A new shift began for me in the early 1990's that would shake my faulty beliefs in eschatology. My early years of traditional dispensational theology gave me a faulty belief system about the end-times and last-days. The result of this shaking was a paradigm shift - to what became a foundational belief that God's original plan was always to come and dwell with and walk with us on earth. I call this the *dominion mandate* – heaven on earth!

It was an uncomfortable revelation, but as I swept away the rubble, I began to see God's heart exposed. God really wanted to bring His Kingdom to earth - as it is in heaven! Jesus really meant it when He told the disciples to pray for the Kingdom to "come on earth as it is in heaven." He demonstrated what it looked like for God's will to be done on earth when He healed the sick, restored the outcast, calmed the storms, raised the dead and set captives free. When He touched the leper, forgave the woman caught in adultery, and loved His enemies. He always planned to have a kingdom of sons who knew that we are heirs and joint heirs with Jesus, His Son. Jesus did not go to the cross so we could endure a long, miserable life on earth and ultimately die and go to paradise. He lived and died so we could have an abundant life now. He has reconciled us and ascended to the Father so we now can come boldly to the throne of God with a heart full of assurance and confidence. That is our Gospel (good news).

> *Death once held us in its grip, and by the blunder of one man, death reigned as king over humanity. But now, how much more are we held in the grip of grace and continue reigning as kings in life, enjoying our regal freedom through the gift of perfect righteousness in the one and only Jesus, the Messiah!* **(Romans 5:17, TPT)**

You and I have now been gripped by His grace and have been called to reign with Him in this life. We are His righteous heirs of salvation and have access to all that belongs to Him. The powerful thing about this is, all the earth and the fullness of it belongs to Him. It has all been created by Him and for Him and He wants to fill everything with himself and cover the earth with His glory through His family. (**Psalm 24:1, 115:16**)

The more I pursued a deeper understanding of the Kingdom of God and began to walk it out, the clearer my understanding of Sonship became. After all, when God sent us the solution to man's fall, it came in the form of His Son. Jesus did not come as the religious, rule-keeping servant and slave, but as a loving and beloved Son who knew His father was pleased with Him. In this, He became the pattern - the model to follow. Jesus did not have to perform or to behave a certain way to *be* His Son. He was born His Son, and all of His thoughts, words and deeds flowed from that relationship. That is our highest calling, to follow Him back to the Father's house.

> *For until the time appointed by the father when he comes of age, the child is under the domestic supervision of the guardians of the estate. So it is with us. When we were juveniles, we were enslaved under the hostile spirits of the world. But when that era came to an end and the time of fulfillment had come, God sent his Son, born of a woman, born under the written law. Yet all of this was so that he would redeem and set free all those held hostage to the written law so that we would receive our freedom and a full legal adoption as his children. And so that we would know for sure that we are his true children, God released the Spirit of Sonship into our hearts—moving us to cry out intimately, "My Father! You're our true Father!" Now we're no longer living like slaves under the law, but we enjoy being God's very own sons and daughters! And*

because we're his, we can access everything our Father
has—for we are heirs of God through Jesus, the Messiah!
(Galatians 4:3-7, TPT)

This is the sign of a heart that has turned - when each of us hears from our innermost being, "My Father – my true Father." When we have trust and faith to receive this, we are no longer slaves to rules or religious rituals. We are no longer covering ourselves with fig leaves of shame and guilt. We are free to be everything He created us uniquely to be. We have access to His heart and to His mind!

As I have already stated, my early experience of faith directed me down a path that led to a very distorted view of God, especially when it came to the idea of God as my Father. It has taken many years of repenting and renewing my mind on this journey to find my way home to the Father's House. I lived much of my early faith from the teachings of my Pentecostal roots. I thank God for this part of my heritage. However, while I was focused on "being filled with the Holy Spirit" for the sake of spiritual gifts, power, and demonstration, I totally missed this dimension of the Spirit of Sonship. The scripture says that the Father sends "sonship" into our hearts **(Galatians 4:6-7)**. This is the key difference that frees each of us from a servant's or an orphan's heart to a secure identity as a son! Being a true son is a matter of birthright, not performance. We have been born into this household of faith – we did not join it like a membership club. Fatherhood is a spiritual matter – so is sonship and the Body of Christ. When Jesus was baptized in the Jordan River, he heard the affirmation of the Father, "This is my beloved Son, in whom I am well pleased."

It is important to note that He had not yet even entered public ministry. This affirmation laid a necessary foundation for the ministry that was to follow. It is vital that all ministry flow from our Father – Son relationship. Jesus was beloved because he was a Son. He had nothing to prove, and neither did we. It is only from our union with Him that we know His heart towards us and those to whom we minister. We cannot release life simply from quoting scripture. We must connect in intimacy with the Father. Then, we will begin to favor him; we will say what He says and do what we see Him doing.

The affirmation of the Father was still fresh in the mind of Jesus as He entered the forty-days of temptation in the wilderness. It is clear that the devil was intent on attacking that thought by asking repeatedly, "Are you the Son of God? If so, then prove it." All the way to the cross, and even as Jesus hung suspended between heaven and earth, the accusatory nagging continued. "If you are who you say you are, save yourself and us!"

When our hearts are fully turned to the Father's heart, we are secure. The heart sees what the carnal mind can never comprehend. When we are living in this level of security, we have no need to perform or to behave a certain way in order to be accepted. This does not mean that our behavior is unimportant. In fact, now more than ever, our lives are no longer our own. *Now, it is in Him we live, move and have our being.* Our lives are governed by a new law, and the name of this law is quite simply called *love*.

As true sons, we have full access to the Father and His house. We cannot earn this access by performing or by keeping the rules. Jesus wanted his disciples to know that they could and would be where He is, not just where He was going. Jesus gave them and us the pattern of true sonship. His heart always surrendered to "not my will but Yours be done, Father", and He calls us to the same surrender. In this surrendering of our hearts, we discover our true identity.

Now we are free.
Now shame is removed.
Now hearts are turned.
Now we are where He is –
safe in the Father's house.

CHAPTER FOUR

Show Us the Father

*Jesus explained, I am the Way, I am the Truth, and I am the
Life. No one comes next to the Father except through union
with me. To know me is to know my Father too. And
from now on you will realize that you have seen him and
experienced him. Philip spoke up, Lord, show us the Father,
and that will be all that we need!" Jesus replied, "Philip, I've
been with you all this time and you still don't know who I
am? How could you ask me to show you the Father, for anyone who has looked at me has seen the Father."*
(John 14:6-9, TPT)

My journey to the Father – son life is not much different than
many I have witnessed. For the most part, once I came to salvation,
I was completely comfortable with my relationship with Jesus.
I was like the Doobie Brothers; Jesus was "just alright with me."
After all, He was always loving the sinners, healing the sick, and
working all the miraculous signs and wonders. Most of all, He
took the death I deserved and did it for me *and as me.* I must
admit, I always loved the way He put the self-righteous leaders in
their place. I liked Jesus, and I knew He liked me.

*Throughout our history God has spoken to our ancestors
by his prophets in many different ways. The revelation He
gave them was only a fragment at a time, building one
truth upon another. But to us living in these last days,
God now speaks to us openly in the language of a Son,
the appointed heir of everything, for through Him, God
created the panorama of all things and all time. The Son
is the dazzling radiance of God's splendor, the exact
expression of God's true nature—His mirror image!
He holds the universe together and expands it by the
mighty power of his spoken word. He accomplished for us
the complete cleansing of sins, and then took his seat on
the highest throne at the right hand of the majestic One.*
(Hebrews 1:1-3, TPT)

As we read this passage, we are enlightened by the true revelation of Jesus as an exact expression of the Father. If we have any view of the nature of God that is not supported by Jesus, our image is not accurate. The key to understanding this relationship is seeing it as it is - a Father – Son relationship.

At this point, I embraced whole-heartedly my salvation and my forgiveness. I accepted Jesus, and He loved me, and because of and through that love, He rescued me. However, as is always the case when our spiritual eyes are busy adjusting to and getting comfortable with the Light we have seen, I did not know what I did not know. I was so focused on Jesus the Savior, that I unconsciously saw Him as not just the Savior from my sins, but the One who saved me from the Father. Unconsciously, I was equating God with judgment and Jesus with grace. I'm not even sure where the Spirit fell in that paradigm, but certainly not as the empowering and guiding force that was about to evolve in my life. I was in my early years of pastoring then, and this evolution fed my ministry as well as the growth of our church family. We found ourselves operating in an almost childlike, naive kind of trust. It opened our hearts and minds to be taught and led in a different way, to honor and to find new life in this understanding of the value of relationship with God the Father and with the empowering gifts of the Spirit.

As my journey continued, I began to see that there was more to my salvation than forgiveness and acceptance because of Jesus. Jesus didn't come to protect me from the Father; He came to connect me to the Father - to birth in me a connection I had lacked for my entire life, both in the spiritual and in the physical world. As my understanding began to open, I saw this idea of relationship and connection with not just Jesus, but with the Trinity in unity - in family - in a collective love, grace and mercy. I experienced the deeper walk that could only be found by adding another dynamic to my faith - the empowering and infilling of the Holy Spirit. At first, this aspect of spiritual life was foreign and a bit weird to me. In fact, some of the believers I observed in this new stream or camp were definitely weird to me. But thank God, my heart was opened to consider and receive what my head could not comprehend. Now, Jesus and I had partners on this journey. A loving and present Father, and an advocate - a representative - a present help.

But when the Father sends the Advocate as my
representative—that is, the Holy Spirit—He will teach

> *you everything and will remind you of everything*
> *I have told you.* (**John 14:26, NLT**)

As this new dimension of my faith developed, the eyes of my understanding began to be illuminated to truth like I had never seen. The most obvious truth was that I was no longer seeing merely from a human and carnal perspective; it was as if my eyes were flooded with light. I was now having visions and dreams. For the first time in my life, I was hearing the voice of God in my spirit – a voice that led me and often chastised me. I was becoming a son in the Father's House, and I didn't even know it.

My lifelong prayer for truth took on a whole new dimension. The scriptures came alive. The gifts of prophecy and healing began flowing through our church. God's supernatural power worked through us. A greater depth of love and compassion took root in our hearts. So much of the foundation I had built my belief system on was based on what I had heard from men who were passing on the same traditions they had received. Not all traditions and heritage are bad unless and until they become idols or forms of bondage to the past or to misrepresentations of the scriptures' intent. In many ways, we were like the scripture says, the blind leading the blind. We were well-intended, but misguided and apt to *fall into the ditch* all the same.

As I learned and grew, I taught and facilitated healthy questions. We sought the Scriptures for depth of understanding. There was a passion renewed. Like David, we began to see this gathering as an opportunity to inquire, to grow, and, ultimately, to learn together. We did not always agree - on the contrary! Even as we questioned, we grew in understanding and in unity. If you want true unity in any group, you have to go through some tough things together. That's how trust and connection are really built. God was among us and showing up in a powerful way, and it was palpable. It was noticeable - even to those who weren't necessarily keyed into a spiritual side of things.

Change of this sort is not easy for anyone. Our reasoning and our understandings, rooted and grounded in decades of teaching, were being challenged. One has to be ready for this kind of change; not everyone can receive it. When a church body is involved in this kind of evolution, some people will go another way, and I remember being troubled greatly when this seemed to be happening with one family that I loved and trusted, a family that had walked in kinship with me in this ministry. There was no conversation about their decision; they were just suddenly absent from our gatherings. I did what good pastors are supposed to do: I visited them, I engaged them in conversation, and I let them know they were valued and needed and loved. Time and again, they embraced me, talked with me, and told me they would see me on Sunday, and time and again I watched for them to no avail.

It hurts when relationships end. It evokes a form of grief with all its stages. To lose a family that has been a part of your work and your vision is heart-rending. Week after week, I watched for them, visited them over and over, and trusted that they would return. One Sunday morning before church, I found myself standing at the window, looking in hopes that I would see their car approaching, when I heard the Spirit say, "Stop chasing goats." It was a powerful and enlightening moment, because it empowered me to release them, to embrace the ministry God was calling me to embrace, and to trust that He would guide them, as well. Letting go is not easy; it hurts. It still hurts. However, chasing goats only compounds the pain and leaves us more confused and hurt than ever. When the Spirit says let go, we must let go. God has a plan that doesn't always fall under the umbrella of our understanding.

It is through difficult times like these that God taught me to hear the voice of the Spirit through which He changed my focus and restructured the core of my entire ministry. One day, I heard the Spirit say to my spirit, *Stop trying to get people to come to church. Instead, love people. Just love people. Go into the community and love people.* And so we did. Within a year, the church was packed. The change in growth came when packing the church became a side effect - an unintended outcome of what our true focus was - loving people.

Many people wonder how we could know it is God we are hearing from or how we could know that the Spirit is truly leading someone who claims to have a message from God? These are healthy and necessary questions. Jesus anticipated this conundrum and gave us a measuring stick by which we could discern such things: "You shall know them by their fruits." I have learned to discern those voices by simply looking at the fruit of the message being declared, as well as the nature of the relationship and the motives of the leader. If I find myself in this place of needing discernment, I've learned to ask myself these guiding questions:

Is there genuine humility?
Am I being nurtured and challenged to think for myself?
Does this person or group welcome hard questions?
Am I being empowered to rise to higher levels?
Am I in a safe place not only to succeed but also
to fall and rise again?

This kind of evolution can be encumbering in itself. I remember the day I closed my bible and said, "No more, God." I was overwhelmed with the opening of my eyes and did not want any more adjusting. Flip on an overhead light in the middle of the night. Harsh light at once, no matter what a gift the light is, can be painful and off-putting. It can cause us to bury our heads beneath the covers and close our aching eyes. This is what I was feeling at that moment, and not just as a believer, but as a minister. How was I going to stand and confess to the people who God had called me to lead that I had been leading them in error? But, I know this, it is impossible to unsee once the eyes of your understanding have been enlightened. Now, I am grateful for the truth I know, although that truth made me angry before it made me free. Sometimes, God will offend our minds in order to pierce our hearts. I now know that I still have more to learn.

For the Lord's training of your life is the evidence of his
faithful love. And when he draws you to himself, it proves
you are his delightful child. Fully embrace God's correction
as part of your training, for he is doing what any loving
father does for his children. For who has ever heard of a
child who never had to be corrected? We all should
welcome God's discipline as the validation of authentic

> *sonship. For if we have never once endured his correction;*
> *it only proves we are strangers and not sons.*
> **(Hebrews 12:6-8, TPT)**

Instruction and correction can feel like abandonment or condemnation if we still carry a wounded, orphan heart. However, knowing the good intention of the Father is vital to receiving correction. It still hurts, and the pain is real, but there is no growth if we run from the process. Eventually, I had to throw off the covers and commit to letting my spiritual eyes adjust to the gift of Light.

When our children are young, we are committed to protecting them, and so it's important to know they are ready for next steps before they do anything that might be dangerous. As parents, we know that these transitions are going to mean an element of failure and struggle as our children learn. When I finally decided that my kids were ready to ride their bikes without the training wheels, I knew for sure that this next phase of freedom was going to come with a cut or a bruise. The moment I let go, a crash was inevitable. Did I want them to suffer? Did I cause them to fall? Of course not! No loving father would feel this way. Neither would any loving father want to protect his child from learning and growing toward independence. We know that there is a level of risk required as riders move toward balance. Could I have prevented their pain? Only by keeping the training wheels in place or by holding on the bike. Having been through the process myself, though, I knew that after a few bumps and bruises, the freedom to ride in the wind and to explore new places would be worth the pain. How we process the pain or discomfort of life, whether it may come because of the Father's chastisement or because of other reasons, is the key to maturity. If we think He is causing the wreck or being negligent, our image is inaccurate.

At the time when God was taking off the training wheels in my spiritual life, I loved to talk to Jesus and about Jesus, and I still do. I loved to pray in His name and in everything try to bring honor and glory to Him. I was amazed at the ability of the Holy Spirit to teach me truth and work through me with divine supernatural gifts. Having dreams or receiving prophetic words to edify the Body of Christ was exciting and fulfilling. The next step in the journey was not as exciting or easy for me. Little did I know that there was still much of the orphan heart still rooted in my soul.

As my dominion mandate, sonship identity and kingdom focus continued to be established in my theology and in my life. I began to see how easy it was for my own beliefs to create just another form of religion, missing the real heart of God the Father. I have felt the correction of the Father guiding me away from "building my own kingdom" and calling it ministry. I know how Abram must have felt when Ishmael, his firstborn in the natural, had to go along with Hagar. I'm sure he was so proud when everyone saw his son and complimented him on walking in God's divine favor and blessing. The only problem was that this was not the favor of God at all. Ishmael was a product of the works of the flesh - Sara's idea and Abram's attempt to fix what God lacked in performing His promise. Ishmael was born out of, and therefore symbolized a lack of trust.

When Philip said, "Lord, show us the Father, and that will be all that we need," the response Jesus gave revealed a profound truth. Jesus pronounced that if we have seen Him, we have seen the Father! Notice that previously, Jesus had said, "I am the Way." The way to what or where? Then He said, "If you want to *come to the Father*, you must come into union with me!" So, it seems obvious to me that the way is simply the way to the Father. Jesus came to reveal the Father. How profound is this idea: A Son came to reveal a Father?

If I were God, maybe I would send an army of angels or lightning to reveal my power. Maybe I would destroy the dragon with a sword or with fire. But no, He sends us a lamb, a Son – an exact image of Himself in human flesh. If you want to see the Father – look at His Son. Look at Him teaching the faithless disciples, kneeling in the dust with a woman caught in adultery, feeding the hungry, opening blind eyes, touching the lepers, healing the multitudes and finally hanging on the cross saying, "Father, forgive them."

It wasn't just happenstance that the old testament closed with a prophetic promise to turn the hearts of fathers to sons and then sons to fathers. This sums up the New Covenant and the order of God's divine plan to restore and reconcile all men back to himself. God sent His Son into the world to save that which was lost - not to condemn the world! The Son came to show us, not just tell us, who the Father really is and how He feels about us.

So if while we were still enemies, God fully reconciled us to himself through the death of his Son, then something greater than friendship is ours. Now that we are at peace with

God, and because we share in his resurrection life, how
much more we will be rescued from sin's dominion! And
even more than that, we overflow with triumphant joy in
our new relationship of living in harmony with God—all
because of Jesus Christ! (**Romans 5:10-11, TPT**)

Many people find it hard to believe that the Father has fully
reconciled us. He made peace with us through the death of His
Son. How much more should we as sons feel secure knowing
that He did all this while we were still his enemies in our own
minds? We have been rescued, reconnected and raised up to sit
at the Father's table.

The Jews were looking for a warrior to come and set them free
from Roman captivity. The Messiah that came according to their
own prophets was not recognized because he came forgiving,
loving, serving, and ultimately dying. This is what reconciliation
looks like. He became human, flesh – an obedient son. He was
the seed that was crushed and was raised up to bring a harvest of
many sons!

But we see Jesus, who as a man, lived for a short time lower
than the angels and has now been crowned with glorious
honor because of what he suffered in his death. For it was
by God's grace that he experienced death's bitterness on
behalf of everyone! For now he towers above all creation,
for all things exist through him and for him. And that God
made him, pioneer of our salvation, perfect through his suf-
ferings, for this is how he brings many sons and daughters
to share in his glory. (**Hebrews 2:9-10, TPT**)

What a powerful truth. Jesus the Son has fully reconciled us, and we have peace with God. We now have access to this new relationship of harmony with the Father. In other words, we can now have the exact connection with the Father that Jesus has as His Son. There are no orphans or stepchildren in His kingdom.

One of the statements that I often heard in my early church years was that God would never "share His glory" with another. In other words, He was holy and righteous and we would never quite measure up and qualify to come into His presence. This scripture clearly says that Jesus the Son has suffered and died in order to bring us into the same glory He had received. So, God has shared His glory with Jesus and those who come into union with Him. This is why we can still say that God does not give His glory to another, yet, He shares it with us because we are not separate, we are the same.

As a leader in the Church for more than 30 years, I see the need for unity in the Body of Christ as vital. But we may have mistaken unity for uniformity. Jesus prayed for his disciples to be one. We often limit this to being in unity and having no divisions among each other. This is admirable and desirable, but I suggest that Jesus meant something deeper. He said, "...give them what I have with you, Father!" Listen closely to this prayer and think in the context of Jesus praying to His Father:

> *Father, I have manifested who you really are and I have revealed you to the men and women that you gave to me. They were yours, and you gave them to me, and they have fastened your Word firmly to their hearts. And now at last*

they know that everything I have is a gift from you, and
the very words you gave to me to speak I have passed on to
them. They have received your words and carry them
in their hearts. They are convinced that I have come from
your presence, and they have fully believed that you sent me
to represent you. So, with deep love, I pray for my disciples.
I'm not asking on behalf of the unbelieving world, but for
those who belong to you, those you have given me. For all
who belong to me now belong to you. And all who belong
to you now belong to me as well, and my glory is revealed
through their surrendered lives. "Holy Father, I am about to
leave this world to return and be with you, but my disciples
will remain here. So, I ask that by the power of your name,
protect each one that you have given me, and watch over
them so that they will be united as one, even as we are one."
(John 17:6-11, TPT)

Jesus was not praying for us to come into some religious conformity and somehow all agree on all things. The pattern God has chosen to reveal His heart, nature and plan is worked out through the Father – Son relationship. Our very salvation is founded on this principle. God so loved the world that He sent His only son. And whoever believes in the son shall not perish. It was this union of the Father and Son that Jesus prayed for us to experience. Jesus did not come to condemn and expose sin; He came to reveal the Father and the true pattern of sonship!

When Jesus boldly tells Philip that seeing Him was equal to seeing the Father, I am sure this raised a few eyebrows. It definitely stirred up a flurry of more questions. In fact, it was this kind of language that caused Jesus great opposition from the religious leaders.

When they heard Jesus say, "The Father and I are one," the Jewish leaders were so enraged that they picked up rocks to stone him to death. But Jesus said, "My Father has empowered me to work many miracles and acts of mercy among you. So, which one of them do you want to stone me for?"

The Jewish leaders responded, "We're not stoning you for anything good you did—it's because of your blasphemy! You're just a son of Adam, but you've claimed to be God!" (**John 10:30-33, TPT**). They interpreted this powerful truth as blasphemy, rather than considering that Jesus might even possibly be who He claimed to be. Herein lies one of the great ironies of the history of the church: Jesus came to a group of people who had been looking for a very different version of a the messiah, and because of their preconceived notions of the person of messiah, when He came, they couldn't see him. The only ones who could see him were those who had not been looking for him at all.

We often find it easy to criticize the religious leaders of the time for this, but modern psychology tells us this is quite common, even today. We are prone to biases we might not even realize we have. Our preconceived notions can completely blind us to the truth (Bellizzi, 2022). The religious leaders of Jesus's day could not truly see Him as the Messiah because he did not fit their vision for who God could be. In this same way, it is very difficult for us to let go of what we've been taught about God and learn to know Him for who He really is.

I have heard it said, "Jesus is perfect theology." I am more convinced of this than ever. Jesus, the Son, has perfectly revealed to us the Father. He opened the door back to Father's House. The family circle has been restored. To the disconnected and lost orphan, I say come on in, there is a place for you. You can have your insecure and wounded heart made whole. Look at Jesus the Son.

> *As for us, we have all of these great witnesses who encircle us like clouds. So we must let go of every wound that has pierced us and the sin we so easily fall into. Then we will be able to run life's marathon race with passion and determination, for the path has been already marked out before us. We look away from the natural realm and we fasten our gaze onto Jesus who birthed faith within us and who leads us forward into faith's perfection. His example is this: Because his heart was focused on the joy of knowing that you would be his, he endured the agony of the cross and conquered its humiliation, and now sits exalted at the right hand of the throne of God!* (**Hebrews 12:1-2, TPT**)

Fasten your gaze on the Son, and you will see the Father! God the Father wrapped himself in the human flesh of the Son in order for us to see His true image and nature. Whatever your view of the Father is, if it is contrary to the life modeled by Jesus, then your view is distorted. Set your gaze on Him, the perfect pattern of our Sonship. He is the perfect expression of the Father's heart.

> *So then, we must cling in faith to all we know to be true. For we have a magnificent King-Priest, Jesus Christ, the Son of God, who rose into the heavenly realm for us, and now*

sympathizes with us in our frailty. He understands
humanity, for as a Man, our magnificent King-Priest was
tempted in every way just as we are, and conquered sin.
So now we come freely and boldly to where love is
enthroned, to receive mercy's kiss and discover the grace
we urgently need to strengthen us in our time of weakness.
(Hebrews 4:14-16, TPT)

Author Leif Hetland addresses this paradigm shift in his text,
Healing the Orphan Spirit:

"We have been taught that God loves us. We also know that
Jesus cares for us. Somehow, the way we understood it was
that if we had a problem, we could go to Jesus, and Jesus
would go to Daddy God and talk to Him about it. Jesus
would make it okay. We also knew that when we came
to the cross, we received forgiveness for our sins. We re-
ceived healing. We received deliverance. But we have never
realized the ultimate goal of Christ was to take us from the
cross to our home with the Father. Our mind could never
see it that way because we had no idea that before the Fall
of Man, we were all part of God's family. We are God's
children....The orphan spirit cannot be cast out. It cannot
be forced out of our systems. It can only be healed. Healing
can only be found in our Father's house. We need to learn
to find our way home. Father is waiting there for us. Let us
come home to Him and experience His love." **(Hetland, 11)**

Hetland's words are a piercing reminder of the prodigal son's
disorientation in the days before he came to himself and

realized that he had a better option - that he needed to find his way home. The message of the parable is clear - that the father is waiting for him, that provision awaits, yes, but so do belonging, acceptance, and true sonship. He has not given up the rights of the family, as he had supposed. On the contrary, his return was cause for great celebration.

When we are struggling or in trouble, we must not run from the Father; we must run to Him. There, we will discover the grace we need to recover and be healed. The Son can relate and identify with our pain and frailty. Let us come boldly and confidently into the Father's house.

> *And you did not receive the "spirit of religious duty,"*
> *leading you back into the fear of never being good enough.*
> *But you have received the "Spirit of full acceptance,"*
> *enfolding you into the family of God. And you will*
> *never feel orphaned, for as he rises up within us, our*
> *spirits join him in saying the words of tender affection,*
> *"Beloved Father!" For the Holy Spirit makes God's*
> *fatherhood real to us as he whispers into our innermost*
> *being, "You are God's beloved child!" And since we are*
> *his true children, we qualify to share all his treasures,*
> *for indeed, we are heirs of God himself. And since we are*
> *joined to Christ, we also inherit all that he is and all that*
> *he has. We will experience being co-glorified with him*
> *provided that we accept his sufferings as our own.*
> **(Romans 8:15-17, TPT)**

My orphan heart began to heal when a vision of the Father's heart toward me finally broke through, past all the biases I carried, past all the emotions that flooded around the very word, "Father". I know now that I have the witness of the Spirit of the Son indwelling in me. I am accepted in the *Be-Loved,* and now that I have seen the revelation of the Father through His Son, I have a clearer image of the Father, myself and all men. And the more I behold that image, the more I am transformed into the same image. We are created to bear His image and likeness. How we see Him will determine how we see ourselves and others. Is He angry, bitter, unapproachable in your eyes? Or is He merciful, loving and touchable?

> *I pray that the Father of glory, the God of our Lord Jesus Christ, would impart to you the riches of the Spirit of wisdom and the Spirit of revelation to know him through your deepening intimacy with him. I pray that the light of God will illuminate the eyes of your imagination, flooding you with light, until you experience the full revelation of the hope of his calling—that is, the wealth of God's glorious inheritances that he finds in us, his holy ones!*
> **(Ephesians 1:17-18, TPT)**

When the disciples said, "Show us the father," Jesus used this moment to give them much more than a mental image. The Apostle Paul prayed this prayer for believers. The original word for illuminate is the Greek, phōtizō. It is where we get our English word, photosynthesis. This is the process by which green plants and certain other organisms transform light energy into chemical energy. During photosynthesis in green plants, light energy is captured and used to convert water, carbon dioxide, and minerals into oxygen and energy-rich organic compounds. In other words, the illumination does not just give vision. It literally causes something to come alive and exist (Smithsonian). We are becoming what we behold. As we get a clearer revelation of the Son, we see the true heart of the Father. As we see Him clearer, we see ourselves in the light.

Can you see Him?

CHAPTER FIVE

Set Your House in Order

Except the Lord build the house, they labor in vain that build it· except the Lord keep the city, the watchman waketh but in vain. (**Psalm 127:1, KJV**)

The idea that a house could be built in vain is alarming to me. The original word vain here implies being *useless, worthless* or *desolate*. The power of the original thought "build the house" is lost in the English translation. The original word used here does not imply construction, but something much deeper. Remember, fatherhood and sonship are spiritual matters, and so is the Church – the house He is building.

The Hebrew word reveals a greater dimension of the house than its construction. It is the word, Banah, that means to *build by obtaining sons or to establish a family*. The only way to build the Father's House – the individuals that make up the church - is by establishing the culture of family and, more specifically, Father – son relationships. This is where the rubber meets the road for many of us. We often *go to church or have church*, but we may be missing the true nature of being the Church – the family of God.

During the worldwide pandemic of 2020-2022, there was much debate about what (and who) was and was not *essential*. The purpose, of course, was to allow for those who were essential to the functioning of the community (and society as a whole) to come out of isolation and to serve the community so that needs could be met. It was a polarizing time, and the remnants of the effects of this pandemic remain polarizing.

In January of 2020, when we had no idea what was coming, the Spirit spoke to me that I needed to reconcile and reconnect. I didn't see it at the time as a prophetic Word, but in hindsight, I can see that God was preparing me for what was truly needed during and in the years following that time. During this time, God spoke to me about being a peacemaker and a bridge builder. Whatever your opinions about whether and how we should have gathered in those days, it is clear that something essential was missing in the days when we were limited in how and when we could safely gather, commune, clasp hands, and embrace.

The rationale for keeping as many people isolated as possible is not lost on me. But we do know that many people who stopped assembling during the pandemic have never returned to any kind of consistent or committed assembling in church. We could have been offended; we could have protested that leaders in our communities labeled the church as non-essential. What is a more revealing indictment on the church is how many believers after the isolation mandates were lifted continued to and, even now, still continue to isolate from the organized church. When our own members begin to see us as non-essential, we have to take a look at why. Could our houses be out of order? Could we be building in vain? Are our gatherings together less than essential?

During one of the most difficult seasons of our generation, why would we dismiss the need for the church? I am persuaded that our cities desperately need the *true church* - not the religious institutions we call the church, but the life-giving, community servants who build up and preserve the family. It is in this family context that we see fellowship and brotherhood manifest as hearts turn to one another. I call it *covenant relationship*. It exists as we nurture and develop a healthy, safe place to care for one another, honor one another and even challenge one another. This is the safest place to fail and find restoration. In the true household of faith, we can completely blow it, as the saying goes, and find the caring heart of a father to pick us up and instruct us on how to recover and move forward. Perhaps this is the true litmus test regarding whether the Lord has built the house. Certainly, that level of safety and grace in churches has not been the experience of many people who are quick to testify against the church today.

The family culture I'm describing is not about controlling or manipulating one another; it is about caring deeply and giving- not just taking. It is about preferring one another, forgiving one another, and honoring one another. It's about what may be some of the toughest commitments to make - to be vulnerable, transparent, and trusting of one another. It's about continuing to love one another.

I have personally experienced this level of relationship with both spiritual fathers and spiritual sons. It is difficult to put into words the peace, joy and satisfaction of giving your heart in a relationship at this level. The personal growth I have witnessed and experienced is nothing less than supernatural. The security and affirmation we all desire as sons can be found only in this context. This level of familial belonging cannot flow out of a superficial commitment. It requires us to be all-in. If we are to find our place in the Father's house and discover our purpose and potential, we must dig deeper than the surface. We must open our hearts and minds to what the Spirit of Sonship looks like.

Unfortunately, when Adam broke the covenant and introduced sin and death into this world, it also introduced shame, fear and religion. I say *religion* because most religions are the manifestation of man's effort to hide or manipulate in an attempt to *make things right*. As we lean on our own understandings, well-intentioned as we may be, there is a devolution of the purity of what is intended as more than just a belief system. What is intended is a familial relationship with God, Himself.

> *Now it came to pass in the third year of Hoshea son of Elah king of Israel, that Hezekiah the son of Ahaz king of Judah began to reign. Twenty and five years old was he when he began to reign; and he reigned twenty and nine years in Jerusalem. His mother's name also was Abi, the daughter of Zachariah. And he did that which was right in the sight of the LORD, according to all that David his father did. He removed the high places, and brake the images, and cut down the groves, and brake in pieces the brasen serpent that Moses had made: for unto those days*

the children of Israel did burn incense to it: and he called
it Nehushtan. He trusted in the LORD God of Israel; so
that after him was none like him among all the kings of
Judah, nor any that were before him.
(2 Kings 18:1-5, KJV)

At the age of twenty-five Hezekiah began to rule. The description of Hezekiah's heart to honor the legacy of King David is literally second to none! There had never been a king like David. Hezekiah was a true reformer and restorer! This is why it must have been devastating when the news came that he was going to die soon:

In those days was Hezekiah sick unto death. And the
prophet Isaiah the son of Amoz came to him, and said
unto him, Thus saith the LORD, Set thine house in order;
for thou shalt die, and not live. **(2 Kings 20:1, KJV)**

The prophet Isaiah offered Hezekiah no hope. It wasn't enough to say he was going to die; he had to punctuate the idea with the assurance that death is the absence of life. What must have felt like, at the very least, an unusual measure of grace was that he gave the king one imperative: "Set your house in order." There isn't much hope in a statement like that.

What in the world could this word mean? What hidden sin was there in the life of Hezekiah? God was warning him, basically, *Death is at the door, so get your affairs in order.* Hezekiah turned his face to the wall and wept. He reminded God that he had always walked before Him in truth with a perfect heart. Apparently, God did not disagree, and before Isaiah could get out of sight, he returned with a fresh word. Hezekiah advocated for himself, and God responded with a promise of fifteen more years. How often do we just accept that things are going to be a certain way without going to the mattresses, so to speak? How often do we just fold our hands and say, "okay", when even God Himself could be persuaded if we were willing to go to Him and plead our case? Isn't this what a trusting son, secure in his relationship to his father, would do?

What did this original word, "Set your house in order," mean? What was out of order? I believe the answer is found in the next chapter:

> *Manasseh was twelve years old when he began to reign, and reigned fifty and five years in Jerusalem. And his mother's name was Hephzibah.* (**2 Kings 21:1, KJV**)

With some simple math, we can understand that at the time Hezekiah was granted fifteen additional years, he had no sons in his house. Manasseh was twelve when his father died. Within three years of the call to get his house in order, Hezekiah did just that; he became a father, and he was granted enough time to see his son through his formative years.

Why would God consider that a king with no sons in his house was "out of order"? For a king, heritage is everything. Who carries on this leadership once the king passes? What becomes of the kingdom? Bearing and training sons and daughters who know how to value relationships with family and with God, who understand that the kingdom is family, and that God is our father, ensures that righteousness follows after we are gone.

Too often we consider current circumstances and fail to advocate for the dream God has placed in our hearts. Often we make concessions, as Sara did with the Egyptian slave Hagar, and in so doing, we produce what only the flesh can produce in place of the promise.

Can we honestly say that what the church is building looks like the House of God? Are we walking in the love and honor of the Father – Son relationship that Jesus modeled? Have we fallen into the culture of the world of business and institutional structures? Do we look more like a civic club than a close-knit family? Do we try to persuade people to join our church, as if it's a spiritual country club? Are we playing a numbers game? A person cannot just decide to join a family; he is born into it. When a heart truly turns, it manifests so much more than attending Sunday meetings and going to church. It manifests a divine plan and order.

How incredible it is that our God is the God who spoke to the chaos and brought the unfathomable creative order that still exists in our universe! All of creation declares that there is a God of intention, design, and order, and this design and order involve letting the Lord build the house—within and among us—guiding the work, letting His grace abound, and allowing the spirit of adoption to join us not only to Him but to one another. In this way, the church becomes the safe and essential place of rest, hope, and rejuvenation for the weary soul—a place where messy people with difficult lives can be safe, connected, vulnerable, and committed to one another and to the growth of the Kingdom, a place of love.

Brenda and I began our pastoral ministry in 1990 with a small group of maybe thirty people. Immediately after I was officially set-in as pastor, the congregation grew to about fifteen. (Yes, you read that correctly.) Over the next three to four years, we began to focus on the outcasts, the addicts, the outsiders and simply preached the Good News and life to the lost. We experienced tremendous growth and pretty much had a constant season of what most church folks call *revival.*

During this season of revival, I spent many hours in prayer and study. Studying back in those days was limited to a few commentaries and a concordance. There was no such thing as Google or the internet for us at that time. We did have some television ministries and radio, but connection and communication were much more challenging than they are today.

I found myself seeing some cracks in the foundation of my beliefs. I had grown up my whole life in a couple different denominational churches. Both were fundamental evangelical and dispensational. The end-times message I had grown up with didn't reconcile with the Kingdom revelation I was seeing. So, I began seeking better answers to the questions that swirled around my head.

What happened over the next year was both wonderful and terrible. Having such a powerful revelation of the scripture, which forced me to rethink and to unlearn was both beautiful and painful for my mind.

This is where we found ourselves. We resigned our first pastoral position and set out like Abram to somewhere God would show us. After visiting several churches for a few months, we finally decided to just have prayer and worship at home and to seek divine guidance as to what was next. Shortly after we began this, without any advertising or invitation, people began joining us. This was the seedbed for what our ministry would become over the next 30 years.

After being in pastoral ministry for a few years, I found myself and our church in a stagnant place. We had a big vision and believed that we were called to change the world with the Gospel of the Kingdom! I was praying and preparing a message about honoring and submitting to godly leadership and authority. I was using the text about the Roman centurion who impressed Jesus with his faith. The man said that he trusted the authority of Jesus' words because he himself was a man with authority and his word carried weight. The key, of course, was that his authority came because he was a man *under authority*, not *in authority*. As I considered this centurion, I became deeply convicted. God was showing me the value of authority at new levels. Don't get me wrong. I valued authority already, but I was preaching to and teaching the people God had called me to lead that they should honor and submit, but that practice was missing from my own walk. To whom was I called to submit? Who held me accountable? Who nudged my thinking? Whose guidance was I bound to trust? At that time, God had brought us into an acquaintance with a fellowship of churches led by Bishop David Huskins. I had only heard him preach on cassette tapes. (Yes, this was a long time ago.) At the time, the message of the Kingdom was being birthed in me at a much deeper level and his voice was like a penetrating knife that spoke to me on a level I had never experienced. We decided to attend the annual fellowship conference and the moment I was face to face with Bishop Huskins, something happened in my heart. I cannot communicate in words exactly what happened, but my heart turned and connected to the voice of a spiritual father.

This covenant relationship released favor and blessings in my life and our ministry for the next 20 years. I found the joy of honoring and serving another man's vision. Many of our dreams and desires were realized, and we entered into a heart-level covenant with one another. He became the spiritual father the spirit had been nudging me toward. Brenda and I connected with a network of churches that were truly family. We have the joy and privilege today of having these same covenant relationships with sons and daughters in ministry. None of these are political or controlling. On the contrary, they are empowering and protecting. Honor and respect are mutual.

> *"And if you are not faithful with other people's things,*
> *why should you be trusted with things of your own?"*
> **(Luke 16:12, NLT)**

Notice the principle here. One of the greatest tests we face in life and in ministry is the test of faithfulness, not just for our own benefit, but for another's. When we walk in these types of relationships, as fathers and sons, we must give our hearts to each other's success. When this is walked out in mutual love and honor, the blessings become multiplied generationally. Instead of being controlled and bound in this relationship, we become free. I found that when I walked in honor and was willing to serve another man's God-given vision, God brought divine favor in my life, empowering me to bring His vision for my life to fruition. I discovered that the voice of God would often come through the man (or woman) of God I had committed to serve. Often the discipline or direction that I needed came as a result of this covenant relationship. While there are many voices in my life, this voice could penetrate my heart like no other. There are many other voices, and I value them, but the voice of the Father that comes in the context of this dynamic will make a baby leap in the womb; the things that are in us that are yet to be birthed will come to life. Their words will quicken our dreams, our calling. The God-inspired desires of our hearts will stir us to action and increase our faith.

In our present culture, covenant is a rare thing. One of the most obvious places we see covenant is in the marriage relationship. A covenant relationship is very different from a contractual agreement. Contracts are legally binding and written on paper. Covenant relationships are spiritual and liberating. They are written on the heart.

Brenda and I have been in our marriage relationship for almost forty years. It is not the power of a marriage certificate or a state-issued license that keeps us together. We have been joined together spiritually and truly have been made one. We have made thousands of choices over and over, again and again, to love and serve one another. It is covenant love and commitment that keeps our relationship strong and healthy. Quitting has never been an option. We are family forever.

As a pastor and a spiritual father to others, I have witnessed this same grace at work in other covenant relationships. It is divine and supernatural what God can do when this dynamic is at work. At the core of covenant relationships is the heart of honor. It exists when two people say, "What is mine is yours. I will sacrifice my comfort and my agenda to see you succeed; your success is my success." Without a culture of family relationship, the house is out of order.

We are in a season of reformation in which God is getting *His House* in order. He is raising up leaders who have the heart of the Father, a heart that will recognize and release sons into their God-given purpose and potential. The Apostolic movement taking place in the world has this "Fathering spirit." Not every stream of this movement is pure, but nevertheless, it is the current flow that God is using to get us in alignment with His order.

The Nicene Creed says, "We believe in one holy, catholic and apostolic church." What is an apostolic message? In order to be an apostolic church, just like the early church was, our emphasis must be on proper relationships in the body of Christ, on fostering unity between believers, on embracing sonship, on the restoration of apostles and prophets, and on the restoration of the authority they should have in the church today. It must be organic and relational – not institutional. Men's egos and agendas must be laid aside. Titles alone are useless and fruitless if hearts are not properly aligned.

God's people are going to see that being apostolic is not "just having apostles," but is the nature of being His people. Jesus was apostolic. He was sent, and we, too, bear His image. The Spirit is preparing the church for greater intimacy with Christ, greater love for each other, greater trust of leaders, and a greater willingness to serve. We come together in apostolic alignment with the many-faceted gifts and callings within the body of Christ, including the five-fold ministry and marketplace ministries.

Part of God's order for His church includes a call to alignment. Anyone who ever assembled a child's toy on Christmas Eve knows that the manufacturer's instructions are vital. There is an order that must be followed. There is an exact place for each part. If you choose to do it your way, even looking at the picture on the outside of the box, you may find the final product is not at all what the manufacturer designed. When we veer from the manufacturer's assembly instructions, we compromise the design of the product.

We have to ward against choosing the order that makes the most sense to us and ignoring God's design for His church. From the start, God's intention for us has been relational. Beyond that, it is familial. God calls us to family. He is our good Father, He values relationships, and in order to protect and preserve this relationship, He has established an order in which we can potentially thrive.

When we see a family that operates in covenant with one another, it is a beautiful thing. They look at one another with compassion. They love with abandon. They have ownership in family goals, and they engage in the work of the family together. They are often very different people with very different personalities, but they see past differences and respect and love one another. When there is pain or injury, they minister to and with one another. It is a rarity in families, and I wonder if it is even more rare in the church. How is it that we get to the point of seeing with compassion and love, no matter the context?

> *"Many prophets were entrusted with all kinds of revelations concerning God's nature – His holiness, love, justice, mercy, faithfulness, wrath and judgments, for example. In fact, over many centuries there was a constant unfolding of revelation concerning His names, the meaning of those names, His nature, His purpose, His love, and His ways. Nevertheless, it was reserved for one particular person to bring the most astounding revelation of all. That amazing revelation is that God is God in Father and in Son - that God is a Father-Son God. But it is not just that God is a father who has a son, but also that God is a son who has a father."* (**Alley J, Kindle Location 635**)

The Father-Son pattern is more than a familial connection reserved for God the Father and Jesus the Son. It is the *order* of how God's restoration plan is experienced by those who come into the Household of Faith. It requires teaching, leading, and correcting. It demands faith, humility - the willingness to correct and to be corrected, to uplift and to be encouraged, to write a promise on our hearts and seal it with active love that does not fail, even and especially, in the face of trying and difficult days. It requires a willingness to see the man or the woman who is not like us in so many ways, and to know compassion and love and to understand that truth that we are powerfully and irrevocably connected. It requires a commitment to build the bridge. There is no exit strategy, *no fifty ways to leave* on a discontented day. We are more than committed; we are walking and living in covenant, and that demands dependence upon one another, respect for one another, the willingness to teach and to be taught, to lead and to submit to one another. It is within that interdependence that we come to a place of empowerment and are able to empower others, as well.

In my reading about fatherlessness and spiritual fathers across society, I came across a book entitled *King Me*. The author, Roger Reeves, illustrated a powerful idea using a game of checkers, expounding on a revelation he had, that when he got as far as he could go he was kinged, and when he was kinged, his borders expanded and his opportunities changed. In the process of playing a simple checkers game, he had a moment of illumination about what it meant to be "kinged" by your father. To be "kinged" was to be mentored - to be taught in such a way that one grows into a king in his own right.

During the exploration of this idea, Reeves talked about how we build bridges to connect and to expand our work. This really spoke to me, and the Lord began to stir my heart with this idea of bridge building. As reconcilers, as connectors, it is vital that we understand what it means to be bridge builders. The purpose of building a bridge is to connect what was disconnected. It is a joining together of two separated places, so that the things and the people on this side can be connected to the things and the people on that side. Being a bridge builder is a daunting and frustrating task. I fully believe that Jesus was the most radical nonviolent reformer in the history of humanity. So, when we are considering social reform, we can look at his pattern - not just of his words, but of how he operated, and his actions can give us insights.

In the tenth chapter of Luke, Jesus was being questioned in an attempt to trip him up, somehow. One of the interrogators pressed Him about the path to eternal life:

> And, behold, a certain lawyer stood up, and tempted him, saying, Master, what shall I do to inherit eternal life? He said unto him, What is written in the law? how readest thou? And he answering said, Thou shalt love the Lord thy God with all thy heart, and with all thy soul, and with all thy strength, and with all thy mind; and thy neighbour as thyself. And he said unto him, Thou hast answered right: this do, and thou shalt live. But he, willing to justify himself, said unto Jesus, And who is my neighbour?
> **(Luke 10:25-29, KJV)**

By countering the same question, Jesus prompted the lawyer to demonstrate that he already had an answer to the question tucked in his pocket, a valid and viable answer. Further, by his follow-up question, we can discern that Jesus knew that the aspect of loving our neighbors as ourselves could be a sticking point. The lawyer confirmed this was true for him when he sought a loophole. I imagine he had successfully used this loophole in his own self- reflection and perhaps with his friends or in discussions in the temple. At any rate, this followup question, "Who is my neighbor?" prompted Jesus to tell a story:

> *And Jesus answering said, A certain man went down from Jerusalem to Jericho, and fell among thieves, which stripped him of his raiment, and wounded him, and departed, leaving him half dead. And by chance there came down a certain priest that way: and when he saw him, he passed by on the other side. And likewise a Levite, when he was at the place, came and looked on him, and passed by on the other side. But a certain Samaritan, as he journeyed, came where he was: and when he saw him, he had compassion on him, And went to him, and bound up his wounds, pouring in oil and wine, and set him on his own beast, and brought him to an inn, and took care of him. And on the morrow when he departed, he took out two pence, and gave them to the host, and said unto him, Take care of him; and whatsoever thou spendest more, when I come again, I will repay thee. Which now of these three, thinkest thou, was neighbour unto him that fell among the thieves?*
> **(Luke 10: 30-36, KJV).**

A current expectation from educational research is that, when teaching a concept or a theory that is abstract in nature, teachers will give both examples and non-examples at once, or if not at once, very close together, so that students can discern the differences and make observations, clarifying for themselves.

(Denton et.al, n.d). This was not an educational trend when I was in school. I love that Jesus was already employing this strategy in his teaching, centuries before, and with great success. I can imagine the faces around Him, particularly that of the lawyer, who had been hoping for a reassuring answer, as Jesus began to establish the context of His story. I imagine them picturing this person, coming from Jerusalem, headed on a journey, beset by violent thieves. I can imagine their eyes, as they picture this man lying prostrate, helpless, robbed, stripped of his clothing and his dignity, his humanity, his manhood, his pride. He didn't get his pocket picked; he was beaten to a pulp and left half-dead on the side of the road. It's a powerful image. At this point, I imagine everyone was actively engaged.

I imagine they saw a glimmer of hope for the man when, thankfully, a priest happened by! Someone whose mission in life was to minister to those in need. Someone who had dedicated his life to serving God by serving others. Were they confused when the priest crossed to the other side, choosing not to help this man? But all wasn't lost. A Levite approached! A Levite, whose job it was to protect others in asylum. Surely, he had experience with helping the helpless. Surely, he had a heart for the hurting. We would expect, of course, that he would stop and attend to the needs of this man. But as His story unfolded, Jesus conveyed that the Levite, also, chose to walk away, leaving the man to die at the side of the road.
What must the audience have thought, hearing this story for the first time? How could it be that both of these men, each with the calling and the empowerment to help the injured traveler, chose to step to the other side of the road and walk on by? They didn't have time for this man at this moment. I wonder if any of

them were quickened, remembering times they had rushed by
a need because of pressing matters. Certainly, the story has
quickened my conscience. We can all rush past a divine
appointment, can't we? "I don't have time for this! I have a
prayer meeting. I have a council meeting. If I am late for
dinner one more time, my wife will let me have it. I don't
have time to get interrupted today."

The audience silently pondered the plight of this dying man. *And
then came a Samaritan.* Talk about a plot twist! This is not something
the audience would have expected. A samaritan! A *half- breed,
illegitimate Samaritan* approached. An outsider! One considered
less-than the Jewish people in all ways. I find it interesting that
Jesus didn't say, "When he saw the Jew…" Rather, Jesus said, when
he saw the *man…*." The Samaritan came to him without prejudice;
he came to him with a response of real compassion.

We know from the encounter Jesus had with the woman at
the well that Samaritans were trained to see the difference in
themselves and the Jewish people instantly. They were trained
and taught that they were lesser. They had been discounted by
the Jewish people, and they had no expectation of a respectful
encounter with the Jews in any context of life. Yet this man
looked at the injured person and saw him as a man; he looked
upon him with the compulsion to help.

He was moved with compassion. No lecture about the dangers
of being on this road alone. No complaining about where he
needed to be or what deadlines he was going to miss. No internal
debate about whether to bother. No instinctual self-preservation

that would lead him, too, to the other side of the road, eyes averted and feet quickened in the dust. No expressions of pity or even sympathy, but true compassion that says, "I see you, and I'm not going to leave you here."

And so he didn't.

The good teacher asks, *Which now, do you think, was the neighbor?*

Indeed, the question is for all of us to answer! Not just in this context, where the teacher lays out two non-examples and an example so that we can clearly see the juxtaposition of good and evil, stranger and neighbor, but in the context of our own lives.

In essence, Jesus was saying that being a neighbor is the expectation of us all. That it has nothing to do with race or ethnicity or neighborhood addresses or familial connections or political alignment. Being a neighbor is a matter of the heart, and its essence exists in how we see one another. The Samaritan did not fail to notice that he was helping a Jew. He did not negate the status of the wounded man on the road, but with his heart and with compassion, he looked past all the barriers that would have kept them divided, and he saw the man.

This powerful story illustrates the true calling of those of us who collectively make up the church. It's important that we get those three, distinct responses to human suffering, because clearly, we can all be tempted to take the path of the priest and the Levite. Truthfully, we can all take the stance of the lawyer in trying to justify our own choices. *Well, who is my neighbor, really?* If we look at those who are suffering with anything other than compassion, if we fail to see the man because we can only see the poor man, the black man, the Jewish man, the gay man, the democrat, the republican…you get the idea. If our view of humanity is clouded by the adjectives we use to define and separate (or to define and join), we can shake our heads in disgust as we read the story of the priest and the Levite, and then fall into that same trap as we travel through life in a different context with different prejudices and different pressures and ideals.

The essence of being a "neighbor" in this lesson Jesus was teaching is truly about eternal life. Not just about being a "good neighbor." It is the essence of Christianity. It should be the connecting thread of the church, itself. When they know us by our fruits, what do they know? When we see others suffering, how do we respond? This isn't a multiple-choice, what-should-he-do kind of question. It's a daily prioritization to which we are called. Consider again the three responses:

> *"…he passed by the other side."*

> *"…he looked at him, and passed by the other side."*

> *"And when he saw him, he had compassion on him."*

The Samaritan built a bridge that day, and when Jesus asked the essential and probing question, *which one, now, do you think was his neighbor.* He was in essence calling us to build bridges that will connect us across any divide. There is no divide too great for God.

Bridges are connectors - pathways. Ways to join what was separated or divided. The Samaritan woman said to Jesus, "We have nothing in common." Jesus built a bridge that let her see and begin to live differently. How untrue it is for us to see another human, no matter who they are or what they do for us, to come to the conclusion that we have nothing in common. It is a dangerous, destructive and prevalent lie.

Several years ago, we went to Nicaragua to build a school. Once we arrived at the place where the school was needed, we discovered that the primary need for building the school was that the river divided the children of that community from where the school currently sat. In addition, every year, children would drown as they attempted to cross the river to get to school. It was much easier for us to build a separate school than to build a bridge. Why? Building bridges is complex, time-consuming and costly. It requires engineering for safety and extensive time and materials to complete. It was much more practical to build and staff an entire new school than to attempt to build a bridge.

Everyone by now is familiar with the Panama Canal, but life was very different before the canal existed. Imagine the great inconvenience it had to be, not being able to pass through or over that seemingly small stretch of land. Someone had the idea to build a railroad to help people journey across. There was a contractor who projected he could build the railway across in about a year for one million dollars. Before the year was over, the contractor was bankrupt and had barely gotten started.

That railroad was eventually completed, but it ended up costing eight million dollars and taking over five years to go forty-seven miles. Further, it is estimated that between five and ten-thousand men died in the process. Once it was finished, a reporter asked what made it take so long to finish, and the spokesman for the railroad conveyed that, in that forty-seven miles of railroad, they built one hundred and seventy bridges. As I read that, it struck me how expensive it is, how costly it is, and how time-consuming it is to build bridges. It's easier for us to just go around, or even worse, just stay isolated where we are. (**History of the Panama Railroad**)

This is true on physical land, and it is certainly true when we consider building bridges across spiritual and societal divides. It will cost us to be bridge builders. It will cost us, and it will probably take more time than we think, and it will be disheartening at times.

As we begin and as we continue this work, we face more than just an internal conflict. Over history, every time reformation has taken place in any way, including in the days of Jesus, there was violent opposition. Not just resistance - violent opposition. I fully believe that Jesus was the most radical, nonviolent reformer in the history of humanity. His teaching to the lawyer and to the others who listened in as he told this story was a radical teaching. It upset all the apple carts in all the circles of society at that time.

In Mark Chapter 5, the scriptures convey a horrific story. When Jesus and his disciples arrived in the area, he met them immediately. The man came out of the tombs. He had an unclean spirit, and the scriptures say that no one could bind him. They often had tried, but he would pluck them off. No one could contain him. Imagine him, night and day, in the mountains, in the tombs, crying, cutting himself with stones, and when he saw Jesus, even from afar, he ran to Him and worshiped him.

This is no parable; Jesus was really there, face to face with this tormented man. Jesus intentionally took the disciples there - crossed stormy waters to get to the land of the gentiles. As soon as they arrived, the scriptures say a man came "with an unclean spirit." The unclean spirit was there, but I think it is powerful to note that the scripture says "a man came." Jesus saw the man. He saw him with compassion and ministered to him and freed him of his bondage. All anyone else had ever been able to do was to attempt to control him by binding him with chains, and even that did not work. Jesus saw the man, and He saw him with compassion, hearing his heart's plea.

> *Until we can see the humanity in all people, we are not seeing with the eyes of Jesus.*

> *Jesus built a bridge.*

> *When Jesus met the Samaritan woman, it was she who brought prejudices to the conversation.*
> *Jesus saw the woman.*

Jesus built a bridge.

When a group of men drug a prostitute down to the temple, declaring that she must be stoned, Jesus had no trouble getting down in the dirt with her - not to justify her, but to make the point that we all must examine our own hearts. They saw her sin. He saw the woman, and He saw her with compassion. He built a bridge.

One of the things that has frustrated me over the last few years has been how I have witnessed men or women of God who should be speaking peace into circumstances and situations seem to be more motivated to stir anger, division and violence. I'm talking about church folks.

Often, we don't know how to process people's pain because we don't have their perspective, and when they try to tell us how they feel, we feel offended because it seems they are trying to blame their suffering on us. "I suffered because of you," they seem to be saying. They are telling us they are suffering, and if we're not careful, we can go into defensive mode.

"I didn't do that." Maybe you didn't, but now it is right there in front of you. You can't ignore it now; it is there. So, now is the time to decide: Do you cross over to the other side of the road and go on about your business, or do you minister to someone who is hurting? Do you find a way to build a bridge? Do you decide, "I need to find a way to connect and to begin to understand your suffering?"
I've had my wounds. I've had my scars. I've had my disappoint- ments. I have suffered in my own way. If you're ever in conver-

sation with someone who can't relate to that, it becomes very clear very fast. *You don't know how I feel or why I feel this way.* In business, I've sat around the table with executives and men of power and influence. I've listened to them discuss theories about what should be done in one situation or another, but I was the only one at the table who had experienced the work in practice. So, though I wasn't in a position of power, my voice was powerful in that context because the practical voice brings wisdom to the conversation. The person who has real, hands-on-the-wheel experience knows something at a different level than those who have heard about it or read about it or theorized about it. This is true in business, and it is true in relationships with people who come from difficult places.

You can read all day about someone's trials, but it doesn't mean you know where they are coming from or what they've endured. The best we can do is see them- really see them- from the heart, with compassion. Build a bridge.

I'm all for the conversation, but I'm also ready to go beyond the conversation; let's reform. We can't have real conversations and real hope of transformation as long as people are burning down houses and attacking one another. There is an onslaught happening in the world. Don't think it's just a physical thing; it's a spiritual thing. It's a spirit that has always been out to destroy the seed of God, the hope of the future. That's why we need to hear the heart of God and speak into the atmosphere, speak into situations the wisdom of God with honesty, with compassion and with heart. We need to stop judging hurting people for not knowing how to reach beyond the hurt. You can't be really conscientious about reform while someone is burning your house down.

Build the bridge. Cross the road. Crouch down in the dirt beside the woman. See the man.

The Church must evolve from being primarily institutional to being wholly relational. Familial. The implications of this are profound. God is looking to move beyond an organizational structure for His people. As outlined in Ephesians 4:11-16, God is working to bring the Body of Christ to complete maturity.

> *And so, dear brothers and sisters, you are now made holy, and each of you is invited to the feast of your heavenly calling. So fasten your thoughts fully onto Jesus, whom we embrace as our Apostle and King-Priest. For he was faithful to the Father who appointed him, in the same way that Moses was a model of faithfulness in what was entrusted to him. But Jesus is worthy to receive a much greater glory than Moses, for the one who builds a house deserves to be honored more than the house he builds. Every house is built by someone, but God is the Designer and Builder of all things. Indeed, Moses served God faithfully in all he gave him to do. His work prophetically illustrates things that would later be spoken and fulfilled. But Christ is more than a Servant, he was faithful as the Son in charge of God's house. And now we are part of his house if we continue courageously to hold firmly to our bold confidence and our victorious hope.* (**Hebrews 3:1-6, TPT**)

Notice that in the new covenant, as opposed to the old, the appointed Son is in charge of God's house. Jesus is our standard and our pattern. He was sent by the Father and was motivated by the love of His father! He is building His church, the house of God, restoring the unity of His family, and we are each an essential part of it. The house is not a building constructed with earthly material or even a mystical place out in the spiritual world; it is the family of sons restored to the Father!

We have built an institution. We have made it about programs and doctrines. It began as a relational connection. We have to accept that we are all on a journey. We are all growing and learning, and we are in different places along the journey. God is bringing us to a full-circle moment in which we see the church as an embracing, covenant relationship. In an institutional environment, there can exist a static and impersonal expectation. People are shamed and shunned and separated. In a relation-based environment, there's room to disagree and to grapple with truth in the context of complicated lives. I feel that is important enough to say again. *There is room to disagree.* How else can iron sharpen iron?

Jesus had no problem letting a demon-possessed person worship Him. How that challenges us! He responded with compassion and mercy, and in freeing him, he upset the economics of the region, and if you wonder what the people of the community valued most, you need only look at their response. Expect opposition. Expect complaints. Build the bridge anyway. See the man. Act with compassion. Seek to understand in moments when defensiveness rises up.

Humanity's cry is not, "Do you have power? Humanity's cry is, "Do you care?" When people are dehumanized, when we class one another, when we discount one another's pain, when we bring our divisions, I just hear humanity saying, "Does anybody care?" We have to do a few things: move from apathy (I don't see a problem) to sympathy (I see enough to feel bad) to empathy (I begin to understand and feel this. I'm listening. I am praying. I am weeping with you) to action (I am willing to cross the road, to get in the boat, to take action with you). When we get to that fourth stage, moved by compassion and operating in love, we will become true bridge-builders.

It will cost us something to build a bridge, but oh the return on this investment! Bridges are not just one-time things. Bridges are cross-generational. They are a legacy and an inheritance. Once someone is willing to build a bridge, then our daughters, our sons, and our grandchildren can use that bridge. No matter what religion you practice, there is an element of love always intermingled, and Christianity is certainly no different, but many people honestly believe it is these days. How do we impact that? Are we showing love? Are we seeing with compassion? Are we seeing humanity? Are we responding to pain as bridge builders? Do people think of love when they hear that we are Christians? God's answer to humanity's suffering was, "Let me come suffer with you."

None of us can change anything in our personal or collective history, but we can change the future. Let us be bridge builders across nations, across ethnicities. Let us rise up as Kingdom citizens. Let us be instruments of healing and restoration. Let us see and love as Jesus loved. This is the essence of the family into which we are called and welcomed by a loving, doting, compassionate Father, and if you are like I once was, you may not have considered that picture of him. Move closer; come and see Him more clearly.

CHAPTER SIX

The Embrace of a Father

"The child who is not embraced by the village will burn it down to feel its warmth"— **African Proverb**

I won't rehash the statistics regarding the effects of fatherlessness on both individual children and on the society in which they struggle to find their footing. I won't rehash that again, except to say that often, we just want a simplistic solution for a complex problem. We just want to "fix" it. In the past year, as I dove into the research about fatherlessness, I was struck by the truth that, often we are not aware of our own dysfunction. Most people who are dysfunctional do not know it; they are living what is normal to them. That's how they are able to stay in that state of dysfunction. When we allow ourselves to live there, we are not living in God's normal.

My personal journey with and through dysfunction stems, not surprisingly, from my childhood, my family, the things that happened or didn't happen in my family, especially as it relates to my father, and I had no idea for years of ministry that my own history had heavily impacted how I saw God - the Good Father.

Mel Wild attends to the connection between physical and

spiritual orphanhood in his book, Sonshift:

> *"First, a spiritual orphan, in a word, is about separation. By definition, orphans are fatherless. Spiritual orphans also live unmindful of being in the constant embrace of their heavenly Father. Their language and how they see and talk about God all reveals this disconnect. While they agree that they are in Christ, God, for them, is up in heaven somewhere while they are on the earth. Therefore, the spiritual orphan mindset is about the illusion of separation. Orphan theology is always about distance and delay."* **(Wild,)**

As I considered the impact of the Father's embrace, the word itself seemed to call to me, and so I took some time to meditate on it, to define it, break it down, analyze it, and see if it would put me back together. Mirriam Webster defines the word embrace in multiple ways:

1) *to hold (someone) closely in one's arms, especially as a sign of affection;*
2) *to accept or support willingly and enthusiastically,*
3) *to cherish,*
4) *to encircle or*
5) *to enclose.*

The root of the word, embrace, is brace. We think of this word in the context of strengthening or supporting something that may be weak or injured. Or perhaps, in the case of correcting, as with the braces we wear on our teeth. How fitting it is that a brace is not intended to shore up our strengths, but our weaknesses. We generally know them as temporary - something to shield or guard to protect some part that is weak or broken until it becomes whole or restored.

I'm convinced that there are some things that need to be healed in our lives that can only be healed when we fully understand the embrace of the Father. Touch is healing. Affection is healing. We live in a culture that historically has feminized affection, often leaving fathers and sons and even daughters unable to cross the divide of discomfort when it comes to being affectionate in word or touch. I struggled with this as a new father, not having had that kind of authentic relationship with my father. How blessed am I that my wife kept nudging me to get past the awkward moments.

> *Scientists have discovered the value of touch in newborns with their mothers. As soon as possible, modern doctors try to get skin-to-skin contact between the baby and its mother. It's because science has proven there are measurable benefits to having this touch as early as possible in life. There's also science that says the hormone, oxytocin, is a great benefit of physical touch. As touch happens, it promotes "good feelings." Oxytocin is literally called the feel-good hormone. It gives us positive thinking and can actually promote an optimistic view of life. Touch measurably impacts the level of compassion we have for others. It also releases dopamine and serotonin in our brains. These substances relieve anxiety, promote healthy immune systems and decrease blood pressure.* (**Rowe, 2021**).

What medical science observes in us can sometimes prove some very deep spiritual things.

God created us this way. God created our brains and our bodies this way. God is pretty smart; the science isn't lost on Him. Consider the value of touch in all of ministry. When Jesus healed the leper (as recorded in Matthew Chapter 8), He did not do it from a safe distance. He reached out and touched him. Unheard of! Unthought of! Certainly not recommended, although the scripture says Jesus touched him, and "immediately his leprosy was cleansed."

In the same chapter, the scriptures tell us Jesus went to Peter's house where Peter's mother-in-law was sick with a fever. Jesus touched her hand, and the fever left her.

In Matthew 9: 27, Jesus was followed by two blind men who cried out for mercy. He touched their eyes and healed them.

When Jesus was training His disciples, one of the ways He said we were to heal the sick was to lay hands on them. *Lay hands on the sick.*

When Paul was talking to Timothy about what had been imparted to him, he said, "Stir up those things that are in you," and he followed with, "They were given to you by the laying on of hands."

John 1:14 tells us the "...*word became flesh.*" Up until this point, God was untouchable. Jesus became flesh so that God could relate. Could touch. Could hug. Jesus could have healed all these people without touching them. There were times when He did such miracles. However, it is significant, I believe, that He made the connection - that He stretched his hand toward them and touched them, and they were healed. Jesus did not do all of this in spite of God's anger toward us. God's desire is to restore fellowship, to reveal Himself to us. God's desire has always been to have an authentic relationship with us, His children.

I'm convinced that there are some things that need to be healed in our lives that can only be healed when we fully understand the embrace of the Father. This is, perhaps, best illustrated through a story that Jesus, Himself, conveyed.

The fifteenth chapter of Luke is one of my favorite parts of the scripture. It begins with an interesting setting:

> *Many dishonest tax collectors and other notorious sinners often gathered around to listen as Jesus taught the people. This raised concerns with the Jewish religious leaders and experts of the law. Indignant, they grumbled and complained, saying, "Look at how this man associates with all these notorious sinners and welcomes them all to come to him!"* (**Luke 15:1-2, TPT**)

The remaining passage records what Jesus said in response to their complaints. I will limit my thoughts here to the part of the passage we commonly call the "Prodigal Son" story. I have come to see this to be more about the running father than the immature, rebellious son.

The son who left the Father's house and wasted his
inheritance was obviously the younger and most
immature. What he discovered out in the world was that
he lost his identity. He joined himself as a foreign citizen.
He became fatherless. Soon, he found himself living a life
of shame and failure. He hungered for a decent meal,
but he would soon hunger for something much deeper.
Humiliated, the son finally realized what he was doing and
he thought: There are many workers at my father's house
who have all the food they want with plenty to spare.
They lack nothing. Why am I here dying of hunger, feeding
these pigs and eating their slop? (**Luke 15:17, TPT**)

He had a desperate need, and when he came to himself, he
knew what he needed more than anything else in the world;
he needed to get back to the Father's house! But, how could
he return with all this crippling shame and guilt? Nevertheless,
he began his journey home.

Imagine the thoughts that must have plagued his mind as
he trudged home, penniless, half-starved, guilt-ridden, and
teeming with shame. How many times did he consider not
even going? I'm sure the thought must have crossed his mind.
Imagine the heaviness of his heart, feet inching toward the
home of his childhood. His mind sifted through explanations
for his mess, the right words to use as he pleaded for mercy,
his willingness - no - eagerness to live as a servant under his
benevolent father's watch. He had accepted that he would never
be a son in the Father's house again. He left with a demand,
"...give me what's mine," and that had been squandered and

strewn asunder. He survived to return, broken and humbled, heavy with the hope of his one prepared plea, "Let me be as a servant."

Shame and condemnation are powerful forces. We should never mistake them with conviction and correction. This broken son was not convicted. He was condemned! Condemnation robs you of any hope of ever being restored to your true identity.

In spite of his shame, the young son set off for home. We know the story, of course, but, envision it with me for a moment, if you will. Allow yourself to step into the shoes and into the frame of mind of that young man, stooped with failure and virtually drowning in uncertainty about what might await. Feel that, and then picture this moment through his eyes, if you can:

> *From a long distance away, his father saw him coming,*
> *dressed as a beggar, and great compassion swelled up in*
> *his heart for his son who was returning home. So the*
> *father raced out to meet him. He swept him up in his*
> *arms, hugged him dearly, and kissed him over and over*
> *with tender love.* **(Luke 15:20, TPT)**

My favorite part of this story is how the Father responded. How he had been going about his daily business when he suddenly saw this figure - the figure of his own son. How, after all this time, and even in his current bedraggled state, his father recognized him, coming from a long distance, and how he raced out to his son, and without word or pause, embraced him. How he fell on the son - literally fell on his neck. How he escorted him…perhaps he even escorted him through the streets, through the crowds, through the gazes of servants and neighbors and family members who must have been agog at the sight. He escorted him through the voices, through the shame, and into the house, and ultimately gave him his robe.

To keep this in context, Jesus is telling this story to religious Hebrews who knew the law. This father, no doubt, knew the law well, and while compassion abounded in the father's heart in that moment, surely his mind was racing with the letter of the law:

> *If a man have a stubborn and rebellious son, which will not obey the voice of his father, or the voice of his mother, and that, when they have chastened him, will not hearken unto them: Then shall his father and his mother lay hold on him, and bring him out unto the elders of his city, and unto the gate of his place; And they shall say unto the elders of his city, This our son is stubborn and rebellious, he will not obey our voice; he is a glutton, and a drunkard. And all the men of his city shall stone him with stones, that he die: so shalt thou put evil away from among you; and all Israel shall hear, and fear.* (**Deuteronomy 21:18-21, KJV**)

Consider the lens of the law at the time when Jesus told this story. It was radical, really. That Jesus would give this story to illustrate how a loving father responds to a rebellious son. At this time in history, if a Jewish son lost his inheritance among Gentiles and then returned home, the community would perform a ceremony, called the kezazah. The whole community would surround the boy, break a large pot in front of him, and yell, "You are now cut off from your people!" The community would totally reject him. So, why did the father run? He probably ran in order to get to his son before he entered the village. (**Kezazah, 2025**)

The father ran — and shamed himself — in an effort to get to his son before the community got to him, so that his son did not experience the shame and humiliation of their taunting and rejection. The village would have followed the running father, would have witnessed what took place at the edge of the village between father and son. After this emotional reuniting of the prodigal son with his father, clearly there would be no kezazah ceremony; there would be no rejecting this son — despite what he had done.

This is such a powerful story, and it speaks to the existence of and the power of a relational God. It is important to remember that Jesus was telling this story to the angry religious leaders who were questioning His character and discernment because He was surrounded by sinners and had been accused of being a friend of sinners. I'm pretty sure that the last thing they expected to hear from him was this story illustrating a God of compassion, undying love, and measureless grace - a God who would drop whatever He had been intent on in a moment and race toward us, burying his face in our necks, and welcoming us back into his strong and forgiving arms. What a passionate love the Father has for those of us who, "like sheep, have gone astray!" Even in the wake of our sins, it is not God's will that we live in shame.

One of the most powerful parts of this restoration story is how the Father went about this entire process. First, we can see that He had been planning this day long before his son returned. He already had the fatted calf; the ring and the robe were waiting. This day had been in His heart and plans all along. Provision was made for this embrace and for restoration to the family this young man had discounted and abandoned in his foolishness; however, the ring and the robe would have done nothing but gather dust had the son not come to his senses and had enough faith to turn toward home.

There are plenty of debates about repentance, grace and restoration happening in our Christian circles today. I will just say that full restoration is impossible without repentance. This repentance required the son to "come to himself" and "return to the Father." He was still his father's son in the pigpen, but the title was of no benefit because his position was one of separation. He had left the Father's house! One true sign of repentance is turning or returning to the Father.

We saw the Father run out to embrace the returning son, and afterward, some powerful images that took place in the house. He did not take the son into some private room and tell everyone to just trust his justice. He put a demand on the others in the house. He sent each of them to prepare for restoration - to fetch the ring, the robe and the shoes. He called on them to prepare the feast and to participate in the restoration celebration. This restoration was a family matter. The Father wanted the son to know that, not only did He embrace him, but so did everyone in the house.

The story also reveals another son in the family that many of us can identify with. The missing son at the party was furious that the young rebel had returned. His orphan heart was also being exposed here. He declared that he had been faithful and pure. He was always working and serving in the Father's house. The problem was that he never left, but he was just as disconnected from the Father's heart as the son who did. He was an orphan in his heart. He failed to see the value of the Father's heart and was always working and performing to feel accepted. He trusted, not in the father's heart, but in the law. Neither do we see any compassion from him or gratitude that his brother was home and alive.

We can only speculate how this worked out, but we have no indication that this orphan son ever accepted the invitation to be a part of the restoration celebration.

What does the embrace of the Father look like?

At the top of the list, it is full assurance that we are accepted and affirmed.

We can trust His heart and His intentions. The Father's embrace is needed most when we fail. We love to have applause and celebration when we succeed, but what about when we fail? It is only in the embrace of a father we find our shame, guilt and condemnation removed. Shame is an unhealthy and heavy weight, and it is not God's will that any of us should carry it, but all of us are subject to feelings of shame, and it can be difficult to know how to move on once we feel we have disappointed ourselves, those who believe in us, or even God. When we are entrapped by shame, it's very difficult to find our way out. Perhaps this is why the prodigal son stayed as long as he did before finally resolving to return home.

> *"We desperately don't want to experience shame, and we're not willing to talk about it. Yet the only way to resolve shame is to talk about it. Maybe we're afraid of topics like love and shame. Most of us like safety, certainty, and clarity. Shame and love are grounded in vulnerability and tenderness. Shame is a focus on self, guilt is a focus on behavior. Shame is "I am bad." Guilt is "I did something bad. Shame is an intensely painful feeling or experience of believing that we are flawed and therefore unworthy of love and belonging. It's an emotion that affects all of us and profoundly shapes the way we interact in the world".*
> **(Brown, 2012)**

> *I write not these things to shame you,*
> *but as my beloved sons I warn you.*
> **(1 Corinthians 4:14, KVJ)**

The Father did not design us to be slaves in His house; we were created to be His sons! The Father does not banish us in shame; He welcomes us back into His outstretched arms.

When I was in those early years of knowing that God had called me to be in ministry, life was not terrible for us. We were not going off the cliff, but I can tell you there was a sense of guilt and a cloud of shame that hovered over my life. There was an emptiness deep in myself. On the outside, everything looked good, but on the inside, I was dying. I was wounded. I was limping along, and I really did not have a context to relate to this Father who was waiting for me with His arms open. It's taken me years to get where I am, but it's only been in the last few years that I've awakened to the fact that so much of our perception of God the Father is so twisted. We think God is angry, and if it weren't for Jesus, He would give us exactly what we deserve. So, we hide behind Jesus, but this entire concept violates the very nature of who God is. Until we see the cross as the mercy and the rescue mission that God wanted for us, until we see God's heart for restoration, redemption and the embrace of each one of us, we are missing it.

Think for a minute of all the things this running Father did not say to his bedraggled son:

- *Where have you been?*
- *Where's the money?*
- *What did you do with your inheritance?*
- *Where have you been?*
- *What have you been doing?*
- *How could you have wasted all you were given?*
- *How could you?*
- *I knew you'd come crawling back.*
- *Why can't you be like your brother?*

The older brother had a list, because he had been at home, keeping the rules. How tragic that he found himself just as disconnected from the father as the one who left. The father, though, simply met his son with open arms.

So now, we can do more than just come to the cross. We can come into the house. Thank God for the cross, but we must not stop at the cross. There is a whole house that the Father wants us to come into. I think the whole world is full of wounded sons, and they are burning down their cities. They are burning down their families. They are burning down their houses. They are burning down their futures because they don't know what it is like to be embraced by a loving Father.

How do we come into the Father's House? We must stop crawling to the throne of judgment when we are called to come boldly to the throne of Grace. You'll never be healed, you'll never be whole, and you'll never know freedom until you know you are free to be you.

When we have healthy father – son relationships, we are positioned for correction and warning if needed. It is not to bring shame or to expose our sin and failures. When we speak the truth in love, it is always redemptive. I have been in the pigpen, and I know the shame and the unworthy feeling of isolation. I have also known the liberation and freedom of the embrace of the Father when I finally came to myself and returned to the Father's house. I have known the healing power and the covering of the Father's embrace. I've seen how He can put a robe of righteousness over my sin and shame, how He never even considers my guilty self-condemning offer, "Make me a slave; I'm not worthy of sonship."

No, He has already purchased the ring. He has already fashioned the robe. The calf is fat and waiting, and no matter how long I've been away, His eyes are attuned to my visage. He knows my walk and the curve of my silhouette. He knows the look of my wilted frame when I am encumbered with shame and dread. He is that kind of Father - the kind who drops all the rules and the expectations of the law and all who care about it, and bounds toward me, falling on my neck and wrapping me in His loving embrace.

CHAPTER SEVEN

The Love of a Father

The beauty and the heart of the story Jesus was telling exists in the value of relationship, specifically in a relationship that was lost and then restored. It is about a son who, through the grace of his father, is restored to sonship and to the household because of a father's love - because a father loved him enough to run to him, to fall on his neck, to cover him. There was no mention of punishment or reprimand. The son was restored in love.

Consider with me another example of restoration from the Old Testament:

> And David said, Is there yet any that is left of the house of
> Saul, that I may shew him kindness for Jonathan's sake?
> And there was of the house of Saul a servant whose name
> was Ziba. And when they had called him unto
> David, the king said unto him, Art thou Ziba? And he
> said, Thy servant is he. And the king said, Is there not yet
> any of the house of Saul, that I may shew the kindness of
> God unto him? And Ziba said unto the king, Jonathan
> hath yet a son, which is lame on his feet. And the king
> said unto him, Where is he? And Ziba said unto the king,
> Behold, he is in the house of Machir, the son of Ammiel, in

*Lodebar. Then king David sent, and fetched him out of the
house of Machir, the son of Ammiel, from Lodebar. Now
when Mephibosheth, the son of Jonathan, the son of Saul,
was come unto David, he fell on his face, and did
reverence. And David said, Mephibosheth. And he
answered, Behold thy servant! And David said unto him,
Fear not: for I will surely shew thee kindness for Jonathan
thy father's sake, and will restore thee all the land of
Saul thy father; and thou shalt eat bread at my
table continually.* **(2 Samuel 9: 1-7)**

The last thing Mephibosheth expected when he awoke that
morning was to find himself welcomed at the King's table. I'm
sure he never considered the value of his father's relationship
with the current king. David and Jonathan's story is one of the
most powerfully covenantal stories in the Bible, certainly in
the Old Testament. David's path had been powerfully impacted
by his own issues with his father; he had been, essentially,
discounted, discarded and discredited by his father and
abandoned by his brothers, after all. Then David came to
Saul, and he at first found connection and relationship, but then
dysfunction followed again because of Saul's insecurities. When
David chose Saul as a father figure, once again he found a dysfunctional father, but David allowed Saul to become a father to
him, and he revered Saul. Jonathan and David became like
brothers, and Jonathan's heart was knit to David. The
dysfunction continued, and it ultimately did not end well, but,
even without the trust and nurturing of a natural father, David
evolved into a man who so valued the role of fatherhood
and the opportunity to be a father to someone. He so valued

his brotherhood with Jonathan that his heart longed to do something to ensure the welfare of Saul's progeny.

Eventually, David found himself in a new place. Saul was gone and Jonathan was gone, and David was on the throne. Everything was settled, but everything wasn't *right*, and David knew that in his heart. His connection to Jonathan remained strong, and, somewhere in his thinking, the need to honor their brotherhood began to stir. So, he inquired about the opportunity to restore sonship to an heir of Saul's for Jonathan's sake.

Mephibosheth had been born strong and healthy - a potential heir to the throne. The scripture tells us that on the day he heard that Jonathan had been killed, Mephibosheth's nurse was carrying him while running, when she lost her footing and fell. As a result of that fall, he was injured and lost his ability to walk. Talk about double jeopardy! The very same day he became fatherless, he also became crippled in his feet.

The world is full of people who are crippled in their walks because they are fatherless, and the church is full of people who should have been carried by nurses and mentors, but who have been dropped, even in a moment of personal crisis. They are mocked because they are lame, but nobody wants to take responsibility for their healing or their provision because, by then, their lives are just too messy. It's a spiritual truth that is often neglected by the modern church, but for Mephibosheth, it was more than a spiritual truth, though it certainly was that. It was a physical truth, as well.

Mephibosheth had lived since the age of five in shame and abandonment - no community, no family, no birthright. By the time David called for him, he was accustomed to living displaced. He knew what had transpired between David, the current king, and his grandfather, the prior king. He knew that, as heir to a former king, he could be considered a threat to the throne. He awoke that morning to the ominous news that the king desired an audience with him. As they brought him to David, he must have trembled at the idea of what might lie ahead.

What a surprise it must have been, not only for him, but to the whole kingdom when the king, seeing Mephibosheth's fear so evident, reassured him that there was no need to be afraid, promising him restoration and provision - restoring to him the land and provision and community connection that had been lost so long ago. Why did David do this? He did it for the sake of his relationship with Jonathan. He did it for the sake of covenant, of brotherhood - of love.

Mephibosheth followed with a question that gives insight into the level of shame he had lived in all of those years. "What is thy servant that thou shouldst look upon such a dead dog as I am?" And David, with a heart for restoration, simply reminded him that he was royalty. I imagine a speech that goes something like this:

"This is Mephibosheth. Son of Jonathan. Grandson of Saul. Today, I restore his land, his heritage, his name. I give him back his legacy. I give him back his honor. I remove his shame. From this day forward, he will always eat bread at my table."

That's what a father does. He takes away our shame. He takes away our reproach. He refuses to let the city elders and the religious leaders shatter our dreams and take away our hope. I think, as fathers, one of the most vital things we can do as we speak and bless and mentor a new generation is to make sure that they never walk in shame. Shame should never be exacted in the name of God. Its purpose is to keep us from coming to the place where we can find what we need. Shame will keep us in a place of unworthiness, struggling with our identity. The most powerful voice in the world is your own, and how we view ourselves and speak to ourselves is paramount to our livelihoods. Mephibosheth needed David to correct his vision of himself. He had been so downtrodden, so discounted that he referred to himself not only as a dog, but as a dead dog. He felt not only inhuman, but completely void of life.

I don't know how long it took for Mephibosheth to see himself differently, but I know that the day came because the scriptures go on to say that he ate for the rest of his years at the king's table, as one of the king's sons, that he had servants who worked his land and served his family, and that he had that which could, if we weren't paying attention, seem like an incidental fact thrown in - a young son, whose name was Micha (**2 Samuel 9:8-13**). Not only had Mephibosheth's livelihood been restored, Jonathan's progeny had been restored.

In Jonathan's absence, Mephibosheth needed a father, and David became that father to him. He knew it fell to him to speak truth over him, to give him a new image of who he was and whose he was. To give him a place at the table was to restore his royal identity, and therefore, to empower him to speak over and guide and pour into the life of his own son, Micha, who would live and walk without shame.

According to the Strong's Hebrew Dictionary, Mephibosheth's name means dispeller of shame. The Oxford Languages Dictionary defines the word, dispel, this way: To make something (especially a doubt, feeling or belief) disappear. What dispels shame? Connection. Provision. Fatherhood. Belonging. Mentorship. All byproducts of what he needed most - the faith and trust of a father.

The further I travel on this Father – Son journey, the clearer it becomes that there has always been a common thread along the way; that thread is love. The desire to love and to be loved is universal. It may manifest in many different ways - even in dysfunctional ways. Nevertheless, it persists as a powerful force in our lives. One could fill a library on the subject of love alone. However, in the context of our subject, let's look at the love pattern of the Father. More importantly, look at how we experience and walk in this love.

Most of us who went to church as young children probably learned a few Bible verses right away. One of the most popular was John 3:16, but many of us did not go further to embrace verse 17, as well. Oh, how the church needs to embrace both verses!

For this is how much God loved the world—he gave his one and only, unique Son as a gift. So now everyone who

believes in him will never perish but experience everlasting
life. "God did not send his Son into the world to judge
and condemn the world, but to be its Savior and rescue it!
(John 3:16-17, TPT)

In order to fully comprehend the Father – Son paradigm, we must see the significance of what the Father intended from the beginning. The creation of the original family in the garden and the response to the fall of man are paramount. It was ultimatly the love of God that created the man with the capacity to choose love and trust. Love and trust had to be willingly offered and accepted. When Adam chose not to trust the heart of the Father, a sin conscience was born and so came fear, shame and, ultimately, death. Adam and Eve were seeking to acquire what was already theirs. They traded their God Consciousness for Sin Consciousness. Swimming in an ocean of provision, they ask for a bucket all their own.

When Adam and Eve made this choice, God's plan was not thwarted. God went to Adam and Eve and asked, *"Where are you?"* In their fear and shame, they attempted to hide themselves. This is one of the sure signs that we are living outside of God's order, when we feel the need to hide ourselves. Shame seeks to keep us in an unhealthy and divided place with one another and with God. Adam and Eve, out of shame for their actions, hid from God in the garden, just as we have a tendency to do in the wake of our failures. This is true for all of us if we let ourselves respond this way. When we come to this place of coming to ourselves and we find ourselves drenched in shame, our initial inclination is to hide.

Having been called out of his hiding place, Adam did what the rest of us tend to do when we've been discovered - he played the blame card. *It was the woman's fault, or it was the serpent's? Or was it yours, God, because You gave me the woman?*

Notice the response that God gave when addressing the serpent:

> *And I will put enmity between thee and the woman, and between thy seed and her seed; it shall bruise thy head, and thou shalt bruise his heel.* **(Genesis 3:15, KJV)**

This is the first glimpse of how the Father intended to bring restoration and reconciliation to what had been lost. He would do it through a seed, more specifically, a son! This is why John 3:16 is much more than a cute memory verse for toddlers. It is the foundation of the Father's plan for redemption, and it includes not just the plan, but the divine motivation for the plan. "For God so loved the world..."

As I began to meditate on the seed (Son) aspect of God's redemption plan, I saw this pattern all throughout the scripture. We saw it with Moses being planted in the house of Pharaoh in Egypt. God hid the seed of deliverance in the enemy's house. We saw it with Samuel being planted in the house of Eli. When Eli lost his vision and refused to correct and restrain his sons, the light in the temple was lost and the voice of God seemed silent, so God sent a seed. We saw David in the house of Saul. Daniel, Joseph, and Ester's stories all offer insight into the methods of the Father to bring restoration from within, with a son!

Mephibosheth's story is such a beautiful example of this pattern. Because of the covenant hearts between David and Jonathan, God did not forget the son who lost his rightful place at the king's table. Mephibosheth's crippled feet were not a result of his own actions; he had been dropped by the one who was responsible for his care.

Now, we can see our part in the restoration process. Jesus the Son was sown in order to bring forth a harvest of many sons. Creation is groaning for the manifestation of the sons of God - not the disappearance of the sons!

> *For all creation is waiting eagerly for that future day when*
> *God will reveal who his children really are. Against its*
> *will, all creation was subjected to God's curse. But with*
> *eager hope, the creation looks forward to the day when*
> *it will join God's children in glorious freedom from death*
> *and decay. For we know that all creation has been*
> *groaning as in the pains of childbirth right up to the*
> *present time.* (**Romans 8:19-22, NLT**)

If restoration is somehow wrapped up in the idea of God's love being demonstrated through sonship, it is vital that we understand the importance of how that love is expressed and experienced.

> *Those who are loved by God, let his love continually pour*
> *from you to one another, because God is love. Everyone*
> *who loves is fathered by God and experiences an intimate*
> *knowledge of him. The one who doesn't love has yet to*

know God, for God is love. The light of God's love shined within us when he sent his matchless Son into the world so that we might live through him. This is love: He loved us long before we loved him. It was his love, not ours. He proved it by sending his Son to be the pleasing sacrificial offering to take away our sins. Delightfully loved ones, if he loved us with such tremendous love, then "loving one another" should be our way of life! (**1 John 4:7-11, TPT**)

The extent of our commitment to love one another is the criteria by which we should measure our true sonship. If we are truly being fathered by God (who is Love), our source of life and love come from intimacy with Him. The real test of authenticity is not how we love Him, but how we love and relate to one another! Love is more than a feeling; it is an active covering that includes healing, cleansing, nurturing and restoration.

The scripture tells us that God *is* love! Love is His nature - His identity. John says that being loved by God is being "fathered" by God. I must say from experience that love is a spiritual matter - the God kind of love. I can also say that fathering is spiritual, as well. We all must know, by now, that having offspring is not the same as fathering. Loving your children, your neighbor, and even your enemies requires something greater than human nature can provide. This is where the love test meets reality. This is where the Father – son life gets real.

If our community doesn't know we are here because we love

them, then we will never reach them with the true message of the gospel. If our fellowship with one another, if our serving one another, if our giving tithes and offerings, does not have at the heart a motive of love, our outreach is ineffective. *"Though I speak with the tongues of men and of angels…"* You know the rest. But do you know the rest? Have you experienced the rest? Have you ministered in the same loving spirit to those God has brought into your lives?

When I talk about the love of a father and how it is that we come to relationship with Him, how we are called to a Father-Son relationship, we have to remember the power of **John 3:16**. God loved us so much that He gave us His son. The scripture doesn't say He lost his son; it says He gave His son. God sowed a Son out of desire for a harvest of sons, and His motive was and remains love.

If how we love one another and relate to one another as brothers is how we experience fellowship with God the Father and Son, it is just as likely that we must discover the value and order of Father and Son life with one another as well. Most Christians have no issue seeing one another in the Body of Christ as brothers and sisters. However, no family is healthy without the recognition and presence of a godly father.

> *That which was from the beginning, which we have heard,*
> *which we have seen with our eyes, which we have looked*
> *upon, and our hands have handled, of the Word of life;*
> *(For the life was manifested, and we have seen it, and bear*
> *witness, and shew unto you that eternal life, which was*

with the Father, and was manifested unto us;) That which
we have seen and heard declare we unto you, that ye also
may have fellowship with us: and truly our fellowship is
with the Father, and with his Son Jesus Christ.
(1 John 1:1-3, KJV)

In this passage, John declared that eternal life - not a long life, but a quality or kind of life - is experienced in a relationship, more specifically, in a father – son relationship. Notice that he also said that it is - not *my* fellowship or *your* fellowship - but *our* fellowship!

The significant qualities and attributes of our relationship with God must be practically walked out in our relationships with each other. I can only give and receive the love of God in my heart by showing it in actions and deeds. It cannot merely be my conviction. If I truly believe, then there should be observable and measurable evidence of that in my life. As I mentioned, we accept this with the brotherly aspect of our place in the family and household of faith, but not so easily with relating to another man or woman as a spiritual father.

I am well aware of the past seasons of what many refer to as the shepherding or sonship movements. I know that there has been, and unfortunately will remain, excess and abuse when pride and arrogance remain in the hearts of leaders. However, we must never abandon truth as a means to bring correction. I once heard someone explaining how banks trained employees to recognize counterfeit money. It struck me that they never studied the counterfeit; they studied the authentic. We need authentic father – son models, so that we can recognize and embrace the real thing.

My journey on this father – son path began as I first discovered many principles of the Kingdom of God. I saw the need to pursue our God-given dominion and cultural transformation. I saw the king and priest identity we have in Christ. I saw the authority of the believer. This is when I also discovered that we have no genuine authority unless we are also *under* authority. I began to see the power of honor and how we not only owe this to God, but to His delegated and assigned leaders in our life.

As I pressed in to better understand this idea of sonship, it became clearer and clearer to me that this was something that had to have fleshed-out, practical application. I discovered that *me and Jesus* did *not* have *our own thing going*; neither did *me and the Father.*

This 'spirit of sonship' embodies certain attitudes, certain values, and certain actions. Principally, this is an attitude of grace we hold in our hearts toward other people, as well as being an attitude of heart toward God. Yes, in Christ we are brought into a dynamic relationship with God the Father and with His Son, Jesus Christ, so we are indeed sons of the Living and Holy One, but we must also learn what it means to live out the values of sonship in the church. We must learn just how to relate to other people with the spirit of sonship in us all the while.

> *"The church is not truly and properly expressing the life*
> *of God in this world unless we are walking in a spirit of*

sonship. Apostolic Christianity is sonship – each of us is meant to be in submission, not only to Christ, whom we cannot see, but also in relationship with those He appoints to lead us. Whom we can see and talk to, and who represent Christ to us. We must be sons to these, our fathers, and in serving them and walking with them, we discover the apostolic life and power of Jesus Christ." (**Alley J**)

I do not write these things to shame you, but to admonish you as my beloved children. For if you were to have countless tutors [teachers] in Christ, yet you would not have many fathers, for in Christ Jesus I became your father through the gospel. Therefore I exhort you; be imitators of me. For this reason, I have sent to you, Timothy, who is my beloved and faithful child in the Lord, and he will remind you of my ways which are in Christ, just as I teach everywhere in every church. (**1 Corinthians 4:14–17**)

Paul was explaining to these new Greek converts that he was not just their teacher, but their father in the faith. The distinction he made here is that teachers or tutors give us necessary instruction; but, fathers are role models we should imitate. In other words, instructors teach what they know, but fathers impart who they are!

"The Corinthians were first-generation believers who had just come out of Greek mythology, which was full of sexual perversion, polygamy, homosexuality and pedophilia. Several Christian teachers were instructing these first-century believers. Yet, Paul had a deep concern that the Corinthian church would exchange (or confuse)

teachers with fathers; so, he sent them one of his spiritual sons, Timothy. What was Tim's assignment? Model sonship for this church that desperately needed fathers. Paul didn't send them a powerful teacher who could give them deep revelation about discipleship; nor did he commission a prophet to foretell their divine family's future. No! He sent them a loyal, loving son so they could observe Timothy's relationship to his spiritual father (Paul) and receive the impartation of the grace they needed to shift their lives from bastards to sons."
(Vallotton, 152)

When we seek to pursue spiritual sonship, it is inevitable that we come face to face with the need of spiritual fathers. This term means many things to different people. Some have seen the misuse and abuse of this idea. Others only relate to the experience of a natural father and project that same perception to spiritual authority. As we think of biblical authority, it is vital that we see it as relational (new covenant) and not contractual (law).

My dysfunctional upbringing planted deep roots of shame, insecurity and lack of trust in my heart. My heart was walled with self-defense mechanisms. I was very competitive and self-reliant. I was an orphan in the Father's house. I certainly could never trust another human as a father. Yet, while I continued to search for significance, security and identity, I could not deny the work the Holy Spirit was doing in my heart.

I would preach or teach submission, accountability and honor only to hear the questions in my own heart asking, *"Who do I walk this out with?"* I would declare that the power of impartation and revelation was available to the sons, but I lacked that type of relationship in my life. I needed the things that only come from a father in my own life. I longed for the love, voice, embrace, instruction, and, yes, *discipline* of a father.

I soon found that God had divinely ordered my steps and crossed my path with the paths of others, and these connections eventually led me to a place of discovery. I found a man whose heart I could trust. I found a voice that unlocked my orphan heart and released me into a greater freedom and security that my mind could fathom. I found deep joy in serving another man's vision. I felt secure in my own ministry, and as our hearts were knit together in service of our Father, I experienced anointing at a whole new level.

Within the umbrella of this father-son experience, I evolved differently as a person and as a leader. My need to validate myself by my performance and achievements began to dissolve. This didn't happen overnight. What we're exploring here became an almost twenty-year journey.

What I learned in that relationship and what I have walked out with my spiritual sons has been life transforming. The spirit of honor and honestly preferring one another brings such deep satisfaction. Seeing a son succeed really is more rewarding than self-success. Having the grace to pray, decree and bless a son and then seeing the fruit come forth in his/her life is indescribable.

Malachi 4:6 begins this way: "And he shall turn the heart of the fathers to the children, and the heart of the children to their fathers…" I have been blessed many times to see that scripture manifest in reality, when a father's heart and a son's heart turn toward one another. It is a joining of the Lord that goes far beyond human reasoning. It is not about being over someone or under someone. It is more like being connected and joined to each other's vision and dreams. It also means being responsible for each other. That's where the security and grace to fail and to recover come in. I have always told my family that the safest place to fall is in the father's house.

I see many today searching for their identity and purpose. Some are succeeding on some level. I was successful at many things. I was good at business and even at pastoring to some degree. What I didn't see at the time was that the success I experienced was built and sustained by my self-sufficiency and self-will. When I began to be healed from my orphan heart and to connect to others in a relationship-based, father-son paradigm, the labor and sweat dramatically decreased. My future and my purpose began to unfold without all the human effort and struggle.

There are many examples of the father-son pattern in the scripture. I have a few favorites.

> *And it came to pass, as they still went on, and talked,*
> *that, behold, there appeared a chariot of fire, and horses*
> *of fire, and parted them both asunder; and Elijah went up*
> *by a whirlwind into heaven. And Elisha saw it, and he*
> *cried, My father, my father, the chariot of Israel, and the*
> *horsemen thereof. And he saw him no more: and he took*

hold of his own clothes and rent them in two pieces.
(2 Kings 2:11-12, KJV)

Elisha had been walking with and serving Elijah for years and became known as the one that poured water for Elijah. From a distance or from the outside, people knew Elisha served Elijah; however, when the time came for transition and succession, Elijah asked Elisha, "What do you want?"

Elisha asked a difficult thing, apparently. He wanted a double portion of Elijah's spirit! What is revealing here is the reference to the "double-portion." You see, *double-portion* is inheritance-based language. The double portion inheritance always went to the firstborn son. So, Elisha was calling out for more than a blessing here. He was calling out for kinship. He said, "I want the blessing that belongs to your son! I want to be identified as your son, not just your servant."

How beautiful that this level of inheritance is exactly what he got! When Elijah ascended out of this world, notice the language Elisha used; "My father, my father." He did not cry, "My prophet", "my pastor", or "my mentor." The relationship between these two men was deeper than that.

There are other examples throughout the scriptures. Moses and Joshua, David and Saul, Samuel and Eli, and in some ways, Joseph and Daniel. One of the clearest patterns can be seen in the Apostle Paul's writings. Paul clearly identifies himself as a spiritual father to the Church at Corinth.

I'm not writing this to embarrass you or to shame you,
but to correct you as the children I love. For although you
could have countless babysitters in Christ telling you what
you're doing wrong, you don't have many fathers who
correct you in love. But I'm a true father to you, for
I became your father when I gave you the gospel and
brought you into union with Jesus, the Anointed One.
So I encourage you, my children, to follow the example
that I live before you. **(1 Corinthians 4:14-16, TPT)**

Paul left no doubt that he considered the believers at Corinth, whom he had fathered in the faith, to be his "sons." He did not hesitate to correct or to challenge them *in love.* He boldly declared that he had this level of responsibility, not based on some religious title, but specifically because of their father-son relationship! I love the way he also clarified that his correction was never meant to bring shame or condemnation! As true fathers step into their proper role, freedom and empowerment will be the fruit, never guilt or shame! A father has the ability to unlock a son's identity. He has the grace to correct or circumcise the heart without wounding the spirit and castrating the ability of the son to reproduce.

Also, notice how Paul differentiates between teachers and fathers. He says that you have endless (ten thousand) instructors or babysitters! They are well known for exposing our faults. This is still true today. We need instructors, teachers and babysitters, but we should never confuse them with true fathers.

I have observed that we are who we are as a result of teaching, training, culture and the grace of God. We have received these teachings on at least three distinct levels. One is by information. These would be teachers or books we get our information from. We can and should gain all the knowledge available at this level. Another level is by inspiration. These would be coaches, mentors and leaders that inspire passion, greatness and desire in us. This level of growth happens in a more personal relationship than you have with the typical teacher or book. Both of these means of growth are natural. Then, there is what I have witnessed as impartation. Impartation happens on a supernatural level. It is spiritual. The affirmation and voice of a father goes far beyond knowledge. Teachers and mentors teach what they know, but spiritual fathers impart who they are.

Fathers bring correction and discipline; not punishment or judgment! Fathers do not simply teach and train by giving information. Fathers inspire and impart who they are instead of what they know. This is why the institutional model of the church will never produce the household of faith as God desires.

> *That's why I've sent my dear son Timothy, whom I love.*
> *He is faithful to the Lord Yahweh and will remind you of*
> *how I conduct myself as one who lives in union with Jesus,*
> *the Anointed One, and of the teachings that I bring to*
> *every church everywhere,* (**1 Corinthians 4:17, TPT**)

Paul wanted to solidify his identity as their father, so he sent Timothy. Instead of coming in person and clarifying his statement, he sent a son. This is powerful. He literally sends them a model of the message. He even says, "He will remind you of me and my ways."

The true test of authentic father-son life is not that we teach a doctrine or take on self-appointed titles, but that we are *always* pointing back to our Heavenly Father. Forgetting this is often the root of the father-son relationship turning abusive. It is proven genuine when we reproduce sons that walk in our ways as we follow Christ. It is when we have imparted who we are in another generation! It is when the orphan hearts are healed that sons awaken to their sonship.

The love of a father is so much more than just an emotional thing. It's okay to feel love. We want to feel love, to feel emotions; however, we can't live our whole lives just responding to how we feel. The love of a father is a commitment. A covenant. Sometimes we find ourselves in a place of deficit - encapsulated in an aching moment in which we realize there is a shortcoming, a deficit, something not right or lacking or missed - some abuse, some void. For me and for many like me, there is no getting it back. My stepfather has been dead for some years now. I can't just go to him and say, "I need this from you." He's gone.

That's what grace is all about. That's where Mephibosheth was. God knew he had those needs. God knows we have those needs. We are not broken because we have the need; we are broken because we don't have the need met. If we are not as fortunate as some, we grow up in a place where anger and judgment are the only responses to our foul-ups. I've wasted and squandered much of my life. I've felt ashamed; however, I also met a running Father, who met me, embraced me, and said, "I love you. You are my son." He didn't stop there. He connected me with a spiritual father in the ministry, who trained me and mentored me and anchored me, who brought me into a new level of maturity, so that I was ready when the time came, to stand up and be that father to others.

The father-son paradigm can be seen in some ways as an order. When we come into alignment and get our house "in order", sons will be born. To be out of order simply means we are out of position. Each of us was created to fit in the household of faith and in the Body of Christ. The fathers have a duty to recognize and nurture each son in discovering and developing his unique purpose and assignment. We will struggle endlessly throughout life, searching for ultimate satisfaction and fruitfulness in the absence of both the affirmation and the direction of a father's voice.

> *We must make this shift in the church if we ever plan to be a pattern for the world to desire. Creation is in travail and groaning for answers. Our present culture is desperately confused about our true identity. Our prisons are full of wayward sons, seeking acceptance and affirmation. "The entire universe is standing on tiptoe, yearning to see the unveiling of God's glorious sons and daughters."*
> **(Romans 8:19, TPT)**

The New Testament is about different realities. It's about the condition of the heart, its longings, its devastation, and its hope for restoration. It's about Christ, who loved us and died for us, about a Father who so loved us that He gave His only begotten son...not to condemn the world, but to save it. And it's about our attitudes toward each other. That is why love is such a strong focus. It's not something we can formalize with a constitution or denominational rules. There is no "love government" or "love council." It is at once vague and difficult to understand or explain and also simpler than anything we've known.

> *"The Church in the world today is changing. This is God's*
> *doing, not that of men. The Body of Christ is changing*
> *from being institutional, denominational and organiza-*
> *tional. It is becoming relational. It is changing from being*
> *centered around formal, organized activities to becoming*
> *centered around relationships and the heart. It's a dra-*
> *matic change of thinking for people – a paradigm change."*
> **(Alley D, 135)**

CHAPTER EIGHT

The Discipline of a Father

Because of the way I grew up, when I thought of discipline, nothing good came to my mind. Nothing. Many, like me, hear the word *discipline* and think of punishment, failure, shame, and disappointment. As a culture, we rarely think of the love inherent with discipline because punishment, chastisement and correction are all unpleasant. Never once have I ever thanked someone for rebuking me. The bottom line is our flesh hates correction. So, if we are not careful, we find ourselves in a situation of wanting to avoid those negative feelings so badly that we fail to have the courage to correct when someone needs correcting, or we fail to have the humility to reflect and receive when correction is offered to us. It's a hard thing. But the scriptures say we should not despise correction, and we have all seen the negative effects on the lives of people who were raised without correction or boundaries and grew up lost and angry, thinking the world should meet their desires. So, in spite of the fact that nobody wants to receive it and nobody enjoys delivering it, we can all agree that correction is a good and necessary part of the familial relationship.

My son, despise not the chastening of the LORD; neither be weary of his correction: For whom the LORD loveth he

correcteth; even as a father the son in whom he delighteth.
(Proverbs 3:11-12, KJV)

It's not lost on me that this scripture begins with the words, "My son." The speaker identifies the relationship before even going further at all. I believe it is impossible to receive, in any kind of healthy way, the correction we all need in our lives unless it comes from someone with whom we have a strong and positive relationship. As sons, we need our fathers to be strong enough to correct us in love. As fathers, we need the wisdom and strength to correct our sons in ways that will truly set them on a better path.

When a father fails to correct his sons, he fails to love them wholly and completely. We have prisons full of our sons in what we ironically call "correctional institutions" because of the massive failure of healthy father – son relationships.

The fear of the LORD is the beginning of knowledge: but fools despise wisdom and instruction. My son, hear the instruction of thy father, and forsake not the law of thy mother. **(Proverbs 1:7-8, KJV)**

According to the Strong's Hebrew Dictionary, the Hebrew word for instruction is mûsâr. It is much more than information and facts; it means to *discipline, chasten or correct.* The thought of discipline is much like the idea of judgment; it seems to always be viewed in a negative light. However, when judgment is seen as justice and a fair verdict, it is really a beautiful thing. So, this is true with discipline when it is experienced in a loving and healthy environment for the right reasons and with respect and love intertwined within a relationship.

"In revealing the Father, Jesus systematically confronted and exposed humanity's false views of God—in particular, the view of God as a punisher who endorses the human punishment paradigm—while revealing His plan to eliminate the punishment paradigm by forgiving sin. For example, instead of participating in the traditional social punishments of the day towards sinners, tax collectors, the ethnically impure, and others considered to be "unclean" or "outsiders"—all of which were justified in the culture on religious grounds—He welcomed them, ate with them, and numbered them among His followers. He rebuked His disciples when they suggested He "call down fire" on a Samaritan village that didn't welcome Him. (Luke 9:52-56). Though "we considered [Jesus] punished by God" (Isaiah 53:4), in reality, Father, Son, and Spirit were working together to absorb both our sin and its punishment and bear them away from us. And they could do this because the paradigm they operate from—the paradigm of love— is stronger than sin and punishment. On the cross, Jesus allowed Himself to enter our sin-distorted view of the Father, to feel our terror and shame, so that He could finally expose that nightmare for what it was—an utter lie—and the truth for what it is—that nothing can separate us from the love of God. In surrendering to death, Jesus was not submitting to His Father's punishment but to ours, while trusting the Father to bring Him through the ordeal of death and back to life again. (**Silk, 60-66**)

In an earlier chapter of this text, I briefly mentioned a football injury I sustained in high school. At that time in my life, my dream was to be part of the in crowd and to be on the football team, and I was all-in. Finally, I reached my senior year, and I was a captain on my football team and a leader among our senior peers. During the second quarter of the fifth game of the football season, the fullback from the other team hit me in such a way that things tore and broke and pulled in ways they were not supposed to. From that brief moment until sometime later, I really didn't know what happened. I think my body went into shock because when I looked at the film later, I saw that I actually fell, got back up, and tried to run, and I had no memory of that. I sat on the sidelines for the rest of the game and finally went to the doctor and to the hospital the following Monday.

The doctor told me that, not only was I done with sports, I would be lucky to walk again. I remember lying there in the hospital a few days after surgery. There was a tube in my leg and my leg had been elevated above my head for several days when a nurse came in and cheerily announced, "We're going to start your therapy today." Without preparing me in any other way, she reached over, slid my feet over the bedside, and let them go. They dropped down to the floor, and honestly, this hurt worse than the initial injury. I let out a yell that was probably adequate to convey the level of excruciating pain I was in, and no sooner had I started to breathe again than she continued, "We're going to take this tube out," upon which she reached down and pulled out the tube, and I released another pain-ridden yell, probably as loudly as the previous one.

"They will be in shortly to start your therapy," she told me before leaving. The therapists came in with instructions and practices that would help me move toward walking again. All of my recovery hurt worse than my injury. They never told me the therapy would hurt, but it didn't take me long to figure out that every part of those disciplines - all of the practices that would move me back toward being able to walk again - would be painful.

One of the reasons we don't embrace discipline is that, primarily, it comes with discomfort. But our growth, our maturity, and the depth of our faith will never be fully realized unless we embrace the discipline of the Father. The nurse was not punishing me. The physical therapists were not punishing me. They gave me what I needed to be able to be healthy and whole again. Had I avoided the pain of physical therapy, I would not be walking today.

As we go through this idea of the father's discipline, it's important that we recognize the Father's heart. The Father's heart is not to punish us. He takes no pleasure in inflicting pain. The Father's heart is not to give us challenges that disqualify us. His heart is to give us opportunities to grow and to mature. What a true father wants is to see his sons and daughters grow up to be healthy, happy and successful, even more successful than he is.

As I grew up in a dysfunctional home, my perspective of a discipline could be summed up in one sentence: Someone was angry or disappointed, and I was going to pay. I can testify to the fact that living in a punishment paradigm adds to the power of an orphan heart. Discipline and correction were never viewed as an act of love in my mind. Yet, the proverb says that when a father delights in his son, chastening and correction are evidence of that love.

Why do we resist correction? Basically, our flesh hates to be disciplined. We hate confrontation and the uncomfortable feeling of being confronted. Our growth depends on discipline, and discipline often comes in the form of discomfort. True fathers are willing to walk through the growth pains in the life of their sons.

The breakdown of the family, and especially fatherhood, has led to staggering numbers of our sons and daughters being robbed of their identity and heritage. The criminal justice system and the mass incarceration statistics make it clear that we are losing generations of future fathers and future sons. When fathers fail to instruct and correct their sons, some structure inside goes undeveloped and the world's system of "correction" has failed us miserably.

The following statistics are gleaned from a 2019 CNN article written by Drew Kann. I have included notations about his sources in an effort to clarify source validity of data:

> "Year after year, the United States beats out much larger countries -- India, China -- and more totalitarian ones --Russia and the Philippines -- for the distinction of having the highest incarceration rate in the world."

According to a 2018 report from the Bureau of Justice Statistics (BJS), nearly 2.2 million adults were held in America's prisons and jails at the end of 2016. That means for every 100,000 people residing in the United States, approximately 655 of them were behind bars.

According to a Prison Policy Initiative report, approximately $80 billion is still spent each year on corrections facilities alone; in turn, dwarfing the $68 billion discretionary budget of the Department of Education."

The United States incarcerates its citizens more than any other country. Mass incarceration disproportionately impacts the poor and people of color. In 1972, there were only 200,000 people incarcerated in the United States; today, that number has grown to 2.2 million.

We have largely moved away from a system that seeks to restore and reform to a system that by design is rewarded for keeping people behind bars. This system is in dire need of reform. On any given day, some seven million people – about one in every thirty-one people – are under the supervision of the corrections system, either locked up or probation or parole (**Kann, 2019**).

Whenever we have a mass shooting or a terrorist attack in our society, the authorities and the media scramble to see what is out there on social media and who these perpetrators are associated with it. The missing question is often simply, "where is the father?"

Just as Jesus is the true pattern of a faithful and obedient son, God the father is the perfect pattern of a father's love. God is love. Love never fails or never ceases. But what does love look like in an authentic father – son life?

> *And have you forgotten his encouraging words spoken to you as his children? He said, "My child, don't underestimate the value of the discipline and training of the Lord God, or get depressed when he has to correct you. For the Lord's training of your life is the evidence of his faithful love. And when he draws you to himself, it proves you are his delightful child." Fully embrace God's correction as part of your training, for he is doing what any loving father does for his children. For who has ever heard of a child who never had to be corrected? We all should welcome God's discipline as the validation of authentic sonship. For if we have never once endured his correction it only proves we are strangers and not sons. And isn't it true that we respect our earthly fathers even though they corrected and disciplined us? Then we should demonstrate an even greater respect for God, our spiritual Father, as we submit to his life-giving discipline. Our parents corrected us for the short time of our childhood as it seemed good to them. But God corrects us throughout our lives for our own good, giving us an invitation to share his holiness. Now all discipline seems to be more pain than pleasure at the time, yet later it will produce a transformation of character, bringing a harvest of righteousness and peace to those who yield to it.*
> **(Hebrews 12:5-11, TPT)**

If we are authentic sons, we will embrace correction and discipline. Yes, it can be painful. No one takes pleasure in being rebuked or chastened. But if we are ever to come to maturity, it is a prerequisite. In fact, my observation over the many years of ministry is that most of the shipwrecked lives I witnessed were those who refused to be corrected.

"Though the words discipline and punishment are often used interchangeably, biblically, they are completely different experiences that produce very different results. Discipline comes from the same word as disciple, which means "learner." But what exactly are we learning? What is the Father's goal in this exchange? He wants to heal us of our wounds, to train us to overcome sin, and to transform our character so that we become mature sons and daughters who look like Jesus. In other words, in the new covenant, discipline is focused on benefitting the person who has made the mess. In the punishment paradigm, the focus is on protecting the interests of everyone but the offender; but in the new covenant, we understand that helping the mess-maker clean up their mess is ultimately what will produce justice and healing for everyone affected by it. Instead of taking the mess away or requiring the mess-maker to deal with the consequences alone, the Father's heart is to walk through the consequences alongside them, bringing comfort, correction, wisdom, and courage as they clean it up. This is His process for helping His children unlearn the punishment paradigm and rebuild their lives in His punishment-free relational paradigm of love, trust, and freedom." (**Silk, 108-110**)

As we look at some examples from scripture, the birth of Samuel and his purpose was very interesting. First, we see a barren woman, Hannah, who desperately desired a son. Her husband could not relate to her desperation. Here was his reply:

> *Then said Elkanah her husband to her, Hannah, why*
> *weepest thou? and why eatest thou not? and why is thy*
> *heart grieved? Am not I better to thee than ten sons?*
> **(1 Samuel 1:8, KJV)**

Notice his reasoning and his question: "You don't need a son; I am better to you than ten sons!" But the truth is, there is no substitute for sonship. All relationships are valuable and necessary, but there is something unusually special about sonship. What I discovered as I pondered Hannah's deep desire for a son was that this was a desire planted in Hannah's heart by God. This was her desire, yes, but it was also God's desire. Hannah wanted a son, and God needed a prophet, and these two facts are beautifully intertwined. The timing of Samuel's birth coinciding with God's plan to bring order to His house is no coincidence.

> *Now the sons of Eli were sons of Belial;*
> *they knew not the LORD.*
> **(1 Samuel 2:12, KJV)**

> *Now Eli was very old and heard all that his sons did*
> *unto all Israel; and how they lay with the women that*
> *assembled at the door of the tabernacle of*
> *the congregation.* **(1 Samuel 2:22, KJV)**

What an indictment on the house of God, especially on Eli, the high priest. It was a tragedy that Eli's sons did not know the Lord. The tragedy was compounded by the fact that he still allowed them to function in the office of the priesthood. Not only were they defiled and corrupt, but they caused the people to follow in their ways.

In the beginning of chapter three, this passage tells us that Eli's eyes had grown dim; there was no vision. The lamp in the temple had gone out. It was the responsibility of the priesthood to keep this light burning and to be the very representatives of God to all of humanity. This priesthood no longer functioned the way God created it in His order, so He raised up for himself a prophet - a son.

The scripture says that Eli lost his vision, and the light went out in the temple.

But long before the crisis appeared, God had already raised up a seed, a son, in Samuel, and He had placed Samuel in the house of Eli. God began to speak to Samuel so audibly that Samuel thought it was Eli speaking. After a few corrections, Eli understood and told him it was God who was speaking to him, and Eli instructed him about how to invite the voice of God to speak. This not only gave instruction to Samuel, it let Eli know that God was connecting with and communicating with this young man.

The young child ministered to the Lord in the temple and suddenly began to hear the voice of God when no one else could. The word that came concerning Eli and his house was devastating:

> *In that day I will perform against Eli all things which I*
> *have spoken concerning his house: when I begin, I will*
> *also make an end. For I have told him that I will judge*
> *his house for ever for the iniquity which he knoweth;*
> *because his sons made themselves vile, and he restrained*
> *them not. And therefore, I have sworn unto the house of*
> *Eli, that the iniquity of Eli's house shall not be purged with*
> *sacrifice nor offering forever.* **(1 Samuel 3:12-14, KJV)**

What a word this young lad had to deliver to Eli. In fact, the scripture says that Samuel feared to tell the word. I can only imagine! But notice the details of the judgment. God said that the purging was a direct result of Eli refusing to restrain his sons and address the sin that he knew about. Eli knew of his son's vile behavior, yet he refused to correct them. Tragedy is always around the corner when fathers refuse to restrain or correct sons. These sons were found to be illegitimate because their father failed to show them the love necessary to bring them into alignment.

So many of the shipwrecks and tragic stories in the scripture can be traced back to the breakdown of the father – son relationship. Another example is evident in the story of Samson. His story is recorded in Judges 13-16. Samson, like Samuel, was born to a barren woman who greatly desired a son, and he was God's answer to a nation in need of a deliverer.

In Judges 14:4, Samson declares his desire to take a young Philistine girl as his wife. Despite his parents urging him to reconsider and marry within his own people, he insisted on marrying this Philistine. The scripture actually goes on to say, "His parents did not know that this was from the Lord, who was seeking an occasion to confront the Philistines; for at that time they were ruling over Israel." **(Judges 14:4, NIV)**

Here we find that the rebellion of Samson began when his father failed to recognize and release his son in the divine purpose of God. To make the situation even worse, when Samson got to the place where he was to marry the Philistine woman he was madly in love with, he discovered that she had already been given in marriage to one of his companions! He did compromise and marry her younger sister. But, he was so angry that he went out and caught three hundred foxes and set them on fire to burn the village, including their vineyards and groves. The Philistines then, in turn, burned his father-in-law and new wife to death. What a tragic story of the man born to deliver Israel! The son that had such high expectations was betrayed over and over and became a man full of bitterness and vengeance.

One other tragic family story we find in scripture is the house of David. The story of David's life actually began with his own dysfunctional family. We see from the beginning that his own father failed to affirm and acknowledge him when Samuel, the prophet, came and requested the presence of all of *Jesse's sons*. David was not *son-enough* to get an invitation, until the prophet probed a bit deeper. We also see how the brothers mocked him when he came to deliver the bread and cheese on the battlefield, just before David stepped up to slay the giant, Goliath. I say all this to illustrate that David's beginning played a huge part in how he actually failed miserably as a father. Not only was David impacted by the way his natural father treated him, he was also greatly affected by how King Saul, as a spiritual authority, treated him later.

Much later in the life of King David, we see the fruit of all this dysfunctional past. Now David had come to the throne, and he ruled the nation well, but not his family. Does this sound tragically familiar?

> *Now David's son Absalom had a beautiful sister named Tamar. And Amnon, her half-brother, fell desperately in love with her. Amnon became so obsessed with Tamar that he became ill. She was a virgin, and Amnon thought he could never have her.* (**2 Samuel 13:1-2, NLT**)

Here we see the unfolding of a tragic series of events including rape, murder and civil war. Amnon set his eyes on Tamar, and lust gripped his heart. Amnon pretended to be sick and asked his father, David, to send Tamar to prepare his favorite dish. She came to serve him and refused his advance, and ultimately, he raped her. Once he had violated her, the scripture says that he hated her more than he loved her. He had her thrown out in the street, where she ripped her virgin gown and put ashes on her head.

> *But now Tamar tore her robe and put ashes on her head. And then, with her face in her hands, she went away crying. Her brother Absalom saw her and asked, "Is it true that Amnon has been with you? Well, my sister, keep quiet*

for now, since he's your brother. Don't you worry about it."
So Tamar lived as a desolate woman in her brother Absa-
lom's house. When King David heard what had happened,
he was very angry. And though Absalom never spoke to
Amnon about this, he hated Amnon deeply because of
what he had done to his sister. (**2 Samuel 13:19-22, NLT**)

There is much in this passage that is heart-rending. David found himself in a situation that would spark outrage in any loving father. Perhaps because of that, the thing that stands out most to me in this passage of scripture is how David responded. We can see that David was angry. What seems to be missing is what David did to correct this situation. The most tragic part of this story is that the father did nothing! Like Eli, David heard and knew that his son raped his daughter. Not only was Tamar's life destroyed, Absalom was now filled with hatred towards his own brother. And what did Absalom do? Nothing at this point. Instead, he let it fester in his heart. For two years, this root of bitterness continued to develop until, finally, Absalom got his revenge and murdered his own brother.

David went into mourning and again failed to bring the loving correction needed to avert such tragedy. Absalom fled into hiding, and the family dynasty continued to crumble. All of this may have been avoided if only the father had been willing to discipline his sons.

Absalom stayed in hiding for three years until, finally, Joab convinced David to bring him home. Just like the prophet Nathan gave David the riddle of the man with one sheep to convict him for taking another man's wife, Joab sent a woman from Tekoa to give another story to open David's eyes. Her story was meant to reveal the King's heart. She had two sons that fought in the field, and one was murdered because no one was there to stop it! Then, the surviving son had gone into hiding because he now feared for his own life. David declared that this son should be restored. Finally, the real-life story became clear. David knew that it was *his* son, Absalom, who should be restored.

It sounds like a setup for a beautiful resolution to a tragic story. However, the problem was actually compounded by the way David approached restoration. He brought Absalom home to his own house, but he refused to have Absalom in his presence. David brought the son home, but he did not deal with the repentance and restoration needed - both for Absalom's repentance and for *his own*. David was still failing to face his role as a loving father, willing to confront and discipline his own sons, and in that spirit, he missed the opportunity for healing. So, what should we expect, knowing what we know about powerful fathers who are disconnected from their sons? We could probably have guessed the next chapter in their story without reading the scripture.

Absalom began his revolt against his father, the King. He sat outside the King's court and clearly stated his case. He told everyone approaching the King's court that they would never get justice from King David! Absalom was still filled with the bitter root of pain and disappointment over the brutal rape of his sister and the glaring fact that his father, *her* father, the *King*, never set things right.

The scripture says that Absalom won the hearts of the people and eventually divided his father's kingdom. It was just a matter of time until David had to face the hard reality that he was about to go to war with his own son. That day did come, and Absalom's army was devastated; he lost over twenty thousand men in one day. Absalom was also killed that day - killed in the woods and buried in a pit:

> *They threw Absalom's body into a deep pit in the forest and piled a great heap of stones over it. And all Israel fled to their homes. During his lifetime, Absalom had built a monument to himself in the King's Valley, for he said, "I have no son to carry on my name." He named the monument after himself, and it is known as Absalom's Monument to this day,* (**2 Samuel 18:17-18, NLT**)

How tragically this story ends. We often see rebellious sons and their disrespect and dishonoring hearts, yet we fail to see the abandoned and orphaned heart that is the root of all this hatred. Absalom was the son of the king, yet he died an orphan. Not only did he live and die as an orphan, he failed to be a father to a son that would have carried on his name.

When David heard the news of Absalom's death, his grief overcame him:

> *The king was overcome with emotion. He went up to the room over the gateway and burst into tears. And as he went, he cried, "O my son Absalom! My son, my son Absalom! If only I had died instead of you! O Absalom, my son, my son".* (**2 Samuel 18:33, NLT**)

In one single cry of sorrow and heartache, David used the phrase, *my son*, five times. How different could this have ended had he used those words before? David lamented to the degree that he saw it would have been better for him to die than to lose his son. But he saw this truth too late - far too late. David saved his kingdom that day, but he lost another son.

We are all responsible for our choices and actions. We should never live our lives as victims of the past. But I can't help but wonder how these stories could have ended if Eli and David had corrected their sons and loved them wholly; they needed fathers who loved them enough to restrain and discipline them.

In our religious systems and in our church systems today, we have similar situations. This idea of discipline and correction is not palatable in today's culture, particularly not in church culture. I'm convinced that there are a lot of things being birthed in the church that are born out of rebellious, selfish, greedy men - men who have not been fathered, who have not been disciplined - men who want ministry to serve them, and fathers who refuse to bring correction when correction is needed. Correction usually comes in the form of a confrontation in which we are challenged. We are challenged, first, to own the fact that there is a lacking in our lives or that we've missed the mark.

We are such a grace-based ministry; our emphasis is on the finished work of Jesus and our identity in Christ, and it is all done and it is all finished, and all of this is true. The only problem is, there are things true of us in our spirits that are yet to be fully formed in our souls. We are righteous, we are holy, we are accepted, we are all of these things. But, sometimes we are selfish. Sometimes we are immature, and none of us enjoy being told that, and, even more troubling, few of us are willing to step up and bring that truth to someone we love, especially when we see that it will not be taken well.

Discipline - correction - chastisement - can be handled two different ways. One dimension of discipline brings shame, pain and reproach. The other brings healing, value and love. They are both based on the same issue, but they are ministered from very different perspectives and out of different hearts. The truth is God has always been at work, molding our hearts, and He has always used others to check our thinking. So many people, of which I am only one, have been hurt. We have been beaten with the Bible, cut with scriptures, and wounded by those who should have been able to help us to heal. There is discomfort in all corrections, but there need not be shame. We are called to correct our sons in love, and many have, instead, taken hold of and administered correction in a way that embarrasses, belittles and separates.

When we have been hurt by that kind of correction, we no longer trust the Father. We get offended, and we leave. We live wounded and defensive and bitter, and now every time someone tries to bring correction to us, we respond defensively. *Don't touch me!* We read the Scripture that says we should not despise correction, but we no longer trust the voice of correction, and so we approach life in self-preservation rather than trust and vulnerability that are required in any true relationship.

One of the biggest challenges we have in the American church today is that we always associate discipline with punishment; we see correction as a negative thing, and, as it is often administered in a negative way, we are met with feelings of push-back - of rebellion - of offense. *Who do you think you are telling me what to do?* When we start to bring the church around to this idea of having fathers, mothers, and spiritual mentors, it brings a huge paradigm shift.

The modern church has evolved into a culture that is no longer comfortable with correction. What we want to do is come to church, give our offerings, hear an inspirational word, and you get me out of here at a good time, feeling good about myself and having been entertained with a few songs. We cannot afford to become a Christian country club, where elders fear correcting and members bristle at correction, and we live and interact on the fringes of acquaintanceship.

That's not what family looks like. Family looks personal. Family rejoices with one another, weeps with one another, struggles with one another and corrects one another. We are called to respect and honor spiritual authority, and that takes humility and commitment *on all sides*. Spiritual fathers' voices in our lives are not about entertainment. We are vulnerable with one another; we welcome relationship and communication, even when the communication brings correction.

Responsibility goes to a whole new level with maturity, and maturity is always the goal when we are bringing up our sons and daughters, whether natural, adopted or spiritual. We want to see our children fully formed and fully developed into what Christ has called us to be. Raising children to maturity requires that we bring corrections when needed. That we bring reproof when needed. That we bring discipline when needed. That we administer all in love. Maturing as sons means that we receive that correction and respond in love.

Years ago in our local church, we did a series of sermons called *Grow Up*. We couldn't give the CD's away. Nobody wants to be told to grow up. Nobody hopes for corrections on Christmas morning; it doesn't really feel like a gift. Yet it is something we all desperately need, and as fathers, we must be strong enough to say, "If you want to be a mature son, this is the right thing. If you want to grow up to be a mature son, this is the right thing. If you want your inheritance, if you want to have influence, if you want to fulfill your purpose in God, there are times you have to discomfort yourself. Deny yourself. Take up your cross. Prefer your brother." Who wants to hear that? These things don't come naturally, but they are necessary in our growth.

We want authority; we want power and dominion, and we were made for all of that. But the journey to that involves having fathers in our lives who will bring boundaries and discipline to our lives. Who brings encouragement and discouragement in wisdom. When I was growing up, the discipline my father brought to me was harsh. I would never say he didn't love me; he was loving me in the way that he knew how, but what it did was to put a root inside of me that became bitter; and my singular thought was, *when I am 18, I am out of here.*

We don't have to look far to see examples of people who have been in this type of father-son environment, in which the voice of the father is the voice of intimidation rather than the voice of affirmation, and it produced servants and slaves, rather than sons. It produced people who were fearful to hear the voice of the father, who feared his approach, especially when they needed correction. It produced, at best, overwhelming and overpowering feelings of shame. Danny Silk wrote a book that really pushed my thinking about this idea of correction. In it, he offers valuable insight about the effects of a shame-based approach to correction:

> *Shame tells us that we are unworthy of connection. The corollary is this: we deserve disconnection. We deserve punishment. This is the belief that fuels human wrath. It's what produces righteous indignation and vengeance toward the offenses of others, and self-criticism and every form of self-destruction in the face of our own. It also fuels hopelessness that people - ourselves included - can change. Behind our efforts to intimidate people into compliance and good behavior, and our striving to create the perception of perfection in ourselves, we are running from a voice telling us we cannot overcome the flaws that make us worthy of punishment, and that eventually, that punishment will catch up to us. Sooner or later...our fear leads us right into the experience we are trying so desperately to avoid. Life in the punishment paradigm is a catch-22, an endless cycle of fear, control, failure, and punishment where we end up saying, like Job, "For the thing I greatly feared has come upon me (Job 3:25, NKJV)."* **(Silk, 26)**

When God wants to correct me, I pray He sends me a true father, one who wants to encourage me and lift me up in that correction. One who wants what's best for me. I pray that, as I serve as a father to others, I am able to correct them in the same way. I know what it is like when the Spirit speaks the truth through human vessels. Whether we embrace this or not, there are things God will speak into your spirit that only you and He need to know about, and that is good. God chooses to put certain people into our lives to speak into our lives. The model and order of father-son relationship has never stopped from the beginning until today. We need the voice of God in our lives.

CHAPTER NINE

The Instruction of a Father: Removing the Shame

We have all heard the phrase, *no one in his right mind*. We apply this to what seems like an obvious choice or direction, and yet, we see crowds of people heading down a path we know will end in shipwrecked lives. How is this possible? This scripture gives us some insight into this:

> *A fool despiseth his father's instruction: but he that regardeth reproof is prudent.* (**Proverbs 15:5, KJV**)

The word "fool" here means perverse or quarrelsome. The idea of the word *fool* as it is used here is of someone who turns to himself for wisdom and understanding and rejects the instruction of his father. The fool is contrary, stubborn and headstrong.

I always thought being headstrong and self-sufficient were great attributes of any successful person. But, I later discovered that I lived much of life as a fool. I never really hated knowledge or learning, but I desperately needed instruction. More specifically, I needed the instruction of a father. A father - son relationship is much more than encouraging words. This connection opens the heart for true authentic conversations and questions. Spiritual heart circumcision requires a vulnerability that does not come naturally or easily. For a son to be willing to expose himself and put his trust in the hands of a father who is wielding a knife can feel terrifying. It is even more difficult for those who have been wounded in the past.

A father's instruction is not just teaching information. There is a spiritual dynamic involved when fathers instruct sons. It is through this process that in-structures are built! When a father takes the proper responsibility of instructing his sons, the inward structures needed to empower and equip sons are supernatural, building the capacity to house the character and integrity necessary to succeed in life. I'm referring to the capacity to create, think, love, forgive, dream and so on. We cannot get this from a book, television or social media. This is only possible with a person-to-person, father – son connection.

I am old enough to remember growing up and going to high school and college before the internet was a thing. Of course, now with Google, Youtube and AI, anyone can find a so-called expert on practically anything. Today, the convenience and accessibility of information is unlimited; however, I fear we have lost the God-created, spiritual dynamics that we experience when we are mentored or apprenticed by loving and caring fathers. The patience needed for that process has all but disappeared. We want our results in minutes, not years. The need for trust and vulnerability has escaped us. As Christians, we see this fleshed out in Jesus' incarnation. God did not send us a book to discover who and what we were created to be. He became flesh and modeled mentoring and discipling at a very personal level.

I cannot recall having any structured or planned methods of instruction from my stepfather when I was a young man. I look back and realize that the majority of my learning came from observing him doing things. There was little explanation as to how or why he went about the things I observed. He was a hard-working man with a short fuse when things didn't go as planned. Looking back in retrospect, I now know that he did much of the things he did because we didn't have the financial resources to pay professional mechanics, electricians, carpenters, or plumbers for the problems or projects that were part of our daily lives. And remember, there was no internet.

One thing I realize now is that I became pretty efficient at those skills myself, simply because I watched him. I have also discovered that not all sons have the same capabilities. Recently, my son asked me to help on a project involving wiring in some electrical wiring. As I was accustomed, I jumped in and started doing the job while he watched. As soon as I began, he stopped me and said he wanted to do it, not watch. He wanted my instructions and explanation of how and why things work the way they work, but he wanted to do the work. He needed my voice in his ear while his hands worked toward the desired effect. It was a teachable moment for me, probably more so than it was for him. After more than thirty years of raising my own children, I saw that I still struggled with my own get-it-done mindset - that maybe I learned more from my father than I thought I had learned as I watched him.

As a business owner, manager, mentor and spiritual father it is important that we have the patience to instruct and empower people to move from hearing and understanding to actually doing things for themselves. This is not natural and comfortable for us as doers. After all, I can do it without even thinking. It will take so much longer if I have to explain all the details and warn of the dangers and watch the process unfold ever so slowly. But, my *aha* moment with Chad that day was powerful because it brought me to a new level of realization - that the goal of instruction is not to get the job done or to be the expert. The goal is to build in-structure that empowers my son to understand and think for himself long after I am gone.

As a pastor and mentor, I have become intentional about teaching people to think. More often than not, whenever I am asked a question, I usually reply with a question, requiring the inquirer to come up with their own answer. Of course, there is the need for dialogue to engage in exploration of the questions that guide us to the answer. But it is more important to get to the deeper thoughts and inquiry mindset than to simply know *the answer*. My own spiritual maturity was extremely limited early on because I simply went to church and listened to the pastor preach, but rarely had the opportunity to question or discuss the message. I don't recall being encouraged to study, pray and search for answers on my own, and I was definitely not going to question the pastor and be disrespectful or rebellious. However, in this mindset as a learner, I missed so much of the joy of learning, of "working out (my) own salvation" (**Phillipians 2:12**), and of finding rich and powerful dialogue with my peers and my elders. Now, I thoroughly enjoy dialogue and even differing opinions. This is how "iron sharpens iron." (**Proverbs 27:17**).

In his book, *Love Your Enemies*, Arthur Brooks said it this way:

> *I have strong views, and you probably do, too. Most likely, we disagree on some things. My point…is not that you need to change your political outlook, but that I need you all the more if you disagree with me, because our disagreement - if we do it right - is what makes our country strong.* (**Brooks, 17**)

> *Brooks, of course, was talking about the political polarization in our country, but this applies to all relationships. In the introduction to this text, Brooks cites research from a Reuters/Ipsos poll, declaring that "one in six Americans had stopped talking to a family member or close friend because of the 2016 election."* (**Brooks, 4**)

How can we impact one another when we refuse to engage? How can we be taught if we are convinced that we have the truth in our pockets? And on the off-chance that we do have that truth, how can we share it if we disengage?

We need one another. Even when we are on the right path with our thinking, we need someone who is strong enough to challenge our thoughts; we need to learn to respectfully disagree and to both receive and be the light as we do so. This is how we grow and connect. This is how we learn. This is how we teach. We are called to do all of this, and to listen, whole-heartedly when instruction is offered.

It is foolish to turn to one's self for wisdom. We desperately need to draw from the wisdom that is deposited in the mature and experienced fathers. It may sound old fashioned, but I can assure you that there are treasures in these relationships that you will never experience watching an expert on a video or simply reading a book. As fathers, we desperately need to turn our hearts toward those in need of this wisdom and experience, and to do so with humility and patience.

A wise son heareth his father's instruction: but a scorner heareth not rebuke. (**Proverbs 13:1, KJV**)

"A *wise* son *hears.*" It all begins with hearing. This is why the voice of a father is so vital to a son. It is like the shepherd and his sheep. There are many voices in this world, but I am convinced that our spiritual ears can hear a level of truth and understanding from our father that is found in no other voice. I have personally experienced this impartation of instruction. I have heard the voice of my heavenly Father speak to me through spiritual fathers more times than I can count. Something awakens in my spirit. Or sometimes it comes as a loving correction or chastisement. Whatever is needed, the key was that I was listening for the instruction, and I embraced it.

I am amazed at the times I have heard confirmation or correction from the voice of spiritual fathers even when they were not aware of my need. I believe this is only possible when we position ourselves to hear. Instead of making a demand for some predetermined direction, maybe we just need to open our hearts and listen. It may come in a casual conversation or a simple text message. We may hear it during a sermon or prophetic word. However it comes, the key is to have an ear to hear.

> *Poverty and shame shall be to him that refuseth instruction: but he that regardeth reproof shall be honored.*
> **(Proverbs 13:18, KJV)**

The dysfunction of living with an orphaned heart brings on one of the saddest things I see so often, the spirit of poverty and shame. So many sons are gripped by these paralyzing spirits. But so many are trapped because they refuse the instruction of a father. Poverty and shame have nothing to do with material possessions; both of these are at their core mindsets. Remember that even an orphan has house, food and clothes but no security or confidence in his sonship.

When we have a poverty mindset, we believe the illusion of scarcity; we live with a level of fear that there is not enough to go around. This produces a *dog-eat-dog* competitive culture in which we see others as a threat to our survival, when the truth is that, not only is there more than enough, but we are created to be creators and producers, not just consumers. As the image bearers of our Creator, there is always more than enough available, and we never have to live in fear of lack.

We can also have a poverty mindset regarding relationships. We can fall into the comparison trap and feel the need to compete for who has the largest following on social media, the most church attendance, or the biggest buildings. The competition isn't limited to these things; the list goes on and on. Relationships should never be measured in quantity, but rather quality! I have often asked people the question, "How many true friends do you have?" By this, I mean, who could you call on in the middle of the night in the midst of a crisis and know that they would drop what they were doing to respond to your needs? Who could you go to with your deepest secret or pain and confide in without being rejected or misunderstood? How many people *truly* know your faults and failures but continue to walk in love with you? How many people have you given permission or access to your life to challenge or correct you if they see the need?

A competitive mindset with regard to sports and economics can be healthy. Strength breeds strength in these venues. But a competitive mindset with regard to growth, talent, and relationships leads to jealousy, distrust and, ultimately, a failure to have the necessary vulnerability to come to each other in love, compassion and brotherhood. A person might have thousands of followers on social media and still have not one friend to call in the dead of night. Which is of more value? What kinds of friendships are we cultivating in our lives? Who could call us? Who knows without a doubt that they could pick up the phone and call us, and we would be there?

We all need that from someone, and we all need to be that to and for someone. That is a true indicator of a deep relationship. When we have a father - physical or spiritual - who will be there, and we have no question in our minds about that, there is a level of trust that is invaluable. We need that father profoundly, even on nights when sleep comes easy and life is teeming with blessings. When the time comes, we need to be prepared to be that father, as well. For some, there was an easy and accessible example growing up. That was not the case for me, but God does not leave us fatherless or without guidance or instruction.

> *Train up a child in the way he should go: and when he is old, he will not depart from it.* (**Proverbs 22:6, KJV**)

Having the instruction of a father is like having a trainer. The word, train here in the Hebrew means to *initiate*, to *narrow* or to *inaugurate* (**Strong's Concordance #H2586**). This gives us the understanding that the scripture really isn't talking about taking their hands and controlling what and how they learn. We need to train a child in the way he should go, that is individualized toward him, toward his gifts, his ways of learning, his needs as a learner - in a way that gives encouragement and strengthens him on his journey.

As a part of a pastor appreciation service a few years ago, Jenn Hilley, who was at the time a member of our church and our praise team, shared a letter to Brenda and me. It was about her learning in the course of her time with us. I love the way she conveyed, with love and with humor, her thoughts on this beautiful process:

> *"Bishop, you have taught me so much, and I love that you truly challenge me to think differently. You always encourage us all to search out the matter on our own. You give me a lot to chew on, and, on that note, sometimes my*

mouth is so full, I can't say amen. You have been so kind
to share your wisdom with me. Brenda, I can't tell you
how amazed I am at your capacity to love; it is ferocious.
Both you and Bishop have helped and are still helping me
through some amazingly difficult situations, but I hope
you know that you have given me the greatest gift anyone
could give. You have given me the peace that truly
surpasses all understanding. You have armed me with the
knowledge that I am redeemed, and being no longer
constrained with fear, my true heart for God is being
exposed. I love you." (**Conference, 2013**).

"Her children rise up and call her blessed" (**Proverbs 31:28
KJV**). As parents, we set our children on a course by blowing
into the sails of their lives. The instruction initiates the
direction, but it does not control the decision process. Sound
instruction gives *throttle*; it sets boundaries. In the simplest
of terms, it directs the path. When we receive instruction, we
grow. Our trust grows, and our maturity grows. While the road
may be difficult, we learn and we grow on the path together.
It is a blessing for both the children and the parents.

But, of course, not all instruction comes when we are ready to
hear it, and not all children have ears to hear. When we choose
to refuse sound instruction, though, we are choosing to be
foolish, and in so doing, we set our own course and often
experience shipwrecked lives.

I will instruct thee and teach thee in the way which thou
shalt go: I will guide thee with mine eye. Be ye not as

the horse, or as the mule, which have no understanding:
whose mouth must be held in with bit and bridle, lest they
come near unto thee. **(Psalm 32:8-9, KJV)**

What a picture! The options here are clear. We can simply listen to and heed the instruction, and the Lord will guide us with His eye. In other words, we have the blessing of being led along the path of life with His vision and not ours. On the other hand, we can be led like a stubborn mule with no understanding, going through life always wondering why and how things turn out the way they do. When we choose this, we choose to let life happen *to* us instead of *through* us.

God rebuked the nation of Judah through the prophet Jeremiah. Notice the language from the scripture:

But they obeyed not, neither inclined their ear,
but made their neck stiff, that they might not hear,
nor receive instruction. **(Jeremiah 17:23, KJV)**

One who refuses the instruction of the father is likened to a stubborn, stiff-necked mule. I pray that we will find the joy of hearing the instruction of a father. Let us no longer be stubborn and stiff-necked. Let us be able to lift up our heads and even look all around and see the big picture - able to see ahead on the path and not have to be dragged down the way, incapable of enjoying the journey, much less the destination.

I don't know why we are so prone to resist instruction, but I know from experience that listening and following the directions of a father can save us much time and heartache. It is like assembling a child's toy or a bicycle we bought for Christmas. All of the parts and pieces are included in the box, along with step-by-step instructions. If we attempt to go with our gut-instincts and start putting together the big obvious parts, we can end up having to take most of it apart in order to get all the small things in place for the perfect product, assembled as intended by the manufacturer. We can save ourselves so much time and effort by simply valuing instruction.

> *I'm not writing this to embarrass you or to shame you,*
> *but to correct you as the children I love.*
> **(1 Corinthians 4:14, TPT)**

The true heart of the Father is bent toward nurturing and developing maturity in His children. Even when we have disappointed Him and ourselves, He cares for us. He nurtures us. In the garden, when Adam and Eve hid themselves, ashamed at the realization that they were naked, God covered them with clothing that He made. God did not want them to live in their nakedness and shame, and He doesn't want that for us, either.

> *Nor would any good father. Current research on shame-*
> *based parenting illuminates a myriad of potential effects*
> *on our children. Children who have been parented with*
> *shame-based strategies are "more likely to be depressed,*
> *drop out of school, (and) be involved in risky sexual behav-*
> *iors, drugs, and alcohol."* **(Rich, 1)**

In legalistic Christianity and dysfunctional homes, shame has had a devastating effect on all, but particularly on our children. Our need to perform or to measure up has created a cycle of unhealthy guilt and condemnation from our leadership, and more tragically, from our own view of ourselves. I know personally how this impacted my life. Most of my drive to succeed and achieve was from the deep roots of shame; from this feeling of never being good enough or measuring up enough, to get the affirmation of a father or anyone I felt the need to impress.

> *Now all discipline seems to be more pain than pleasure at the time, yet later it will produce a transformation of character, bringing a harvest of righteousness and peace to those who yield to it.* (**Hebrews 12:1, 3-8, 11, TPT**)

"The first thing to notice here is that in the new covenant, discipline is a relational exchange between the Father and His children. Though in the body of Christ, we do experience discipline through human authority figures like parents and leaders; that discipline is only functioning correctly when those figures accurately represent the heart of the Father and lead and equip people to connect more deeply with Him. Every discipline scenario is first and foremost about this relationship.

> *The second thing to see is the Father's goal in this exchange. He wants to heal us of our wounds, train us to overcome sin, and transform our character so that we become mature sons and daughters who look like Jesus. In other words, in the new covenant, discipline is focused on benefitting the person who has made the mess.*
> *In the punishment paradigm, the focus is on protecting*

the interests of everyone but the offender, but in the new
covenant, we understand that helping the mess-maker
clean up their mess is ultimately what will produce justice
and healing for everyone affected by it. Instead of
taking the mess away or requiring the mess-maker to deal
with the consequences alone, the Father's heart is to walk
through the consequences alongside them, bringing
comfort, correction, wisdom, and courage as they clean
it up. This is His process for helping His kids unlearn the
punishment paradigm and rebuild their lives in His
punishment-free relational paradigm of love, trust, and
freedom. Where else can He best show us that His heart is
not to punish us, but to remove our shame, forgive us, free
us from the fear of punishment, and lead us into loving,
safe connection with Him than in our messes
and mistakes? Where else can we best grow and learn
than by seeing our Father redeem our failures and
use them to make us wise?" **(Silk, 78-79)**

Let's return for a minute to the previous story about King
David, Amnon, Tamar and Absalom. In this, we have insight
about the failure of King David to discipline his sons, which
eventually created a household of victims. I would submit that
the greatest victim in the entire story was Tamar. She was raped
by her own half-brother, Amnon, who then rejected her and
blamed her for the entire thing. Then her other half-brother,
Absalom, hid her away and basically told her to be quiet and not
embarrass the royal family. Her father, David, was outraged but
did nothing to confront the issue or to hold Amnon accountable.

Her brother Absalom saw her and asked, "Is it true that Amnon has been with you? Well, my sister, keep quiet for now, since he's your brother. Don't you worry about it." So, Tamar lived as a desolate woman in her brother Absalom's house. (**2 Samuel 13:20, NLT**)

What a tragic way to deal with all the pain Tamar was facing! *Just be quiet.* Whenever we refuse to deal with the pain or place the guilt where it rightly belongs, we bury these feelings deep within, and the shame only gets worse over time. Worse yet, the shame often gets displaced, as it did with Tamar. How sad are the words, "Tamar lived as a desolate woman." We have no record that Tamar ever recovered her dignity. We know that just keeping quiet only fueled the anger and hatred in the heart of Absalom. He kept quiet for over two years and finally carried out the murder that developed in his heart against Amnon.

After this, King David repeated the pattern yet again, sending Absalom away and refusing to even see his face for three years. Finally, after burying the shame and avoiding the issue, Absalom ultimately stirred up a rebellion against the King that divided the nation and, ultimately, led to his own death.

We often hear of the *Absalom spirit* as a rebellious spirit. Even that seems an unfair judgment, given that, in all of this, Absalom was the only one who really wanted to address the issues of dysfunctions in the family. It was he who took Tamar in. He was a daily witness to her mourning. The juxtaposition of his memory of her, free and beautiful, to this desolate woman she had become. No doubt, he felt the weight of her sorrow and disillusionment more profoundly than anyone; so profoundly that he eventually burned with the need for revenge, acted on it, and brought even more devastation to the family. Whenever a father fails in this way, we often see sons act out in a desperate cry for healing, honesty and justice. How could David be so blind? How could he not see the shame, anger and pain in his own house?

The roots of shame can be seen in our earliest introduction of David, the shepherd boy. Whenever the prophet Samuel came to anoint one of Jesse's sons to be the next king, David was not even invited to the meeting. How he must have felt knowing that when his father was presenting his sons for such a monumental occasion, he was not included. Even after the prophet affirmed him, scripture records no celebration from the father or his brothers. God's plan for David went so far beyond the family's vision of who he was, they couldn't embrace it.

When David went out to face Goliath and delivered the nation in a single battle, his brothers still refused to recognize the anointing on his life. Yet, David remained silent. We find no recording of him boasting of this victory or standing up for himself to his brothers. He did what he had been taught to do; he coped with his shame by pressing it further and further down inside.

When David committed adultery with Bathsheba and subsequently learned of her pregnancy, his priority was to cover up his sin. The simplest solution was to bring her husband, Uriah, home to spend a night with her. All David needed was for Uriah to return home from battle and sleep with his wife and, thereby, cover up his sin. But David's plan backfired. Uriah was an honorable man, and he refused to sleep with his own wife while his brothers were in battle.

Faced with this stumbling block, David's priority did not change. The chief thing on his mind was covering up his sin. So, in order to keep things secret, David had Uriah led to the front of the line to die in battle. David was so committed to covering up his sin that he was willing to have an honorable and loyal man killed in order to do it.

This pattern of avoiding the issues had a long history in David's family, and he had fallen into the trap of repeating what he had lived before. He seemed to have no context for honest transparency and openly dealing with shame and pain. Even after the prophet Nathan confronted David and he quickly repented, we see another sign that David was not good with dealing with the inner turmoil of grief and shame.

The child conceived and born in this scandalous affair is sick, and David shuts himself in to pray and fast.

> *David begged God to spare the child. He went without food and lay all night on the bare ground. The elders of his household pleaded with him to get up and eat with them, but he refused. Then on the seventh day the child died. David's advisers were afraid to tell him. "He wouldn't listen to reason while the child was ill," they said. "What*

drastic thing will he do when we tell him the child is dead?" When David saw them whispering, he realized what had happened. "Is the child dead?" he asked. "Yes," they replied, "he is dead." Then David got up from the ground, washed himself, put on lotions, and changed his clothes. He went to the Tabernacle and worshiped the LORD. After that, he returned to the palace and was served food and ate. His advisers were amazed. "We don't understand you," they told him. "While the child was still living, you wept and refused to eat. But now that the child is dead, you have stopped your mourning and are eating again." David replied, "I fasted and wept while the child was alive, for I said, 'Perhaps the LORD will be gracious to me and let the child live.' But why should I fast when he is dead? Can I bring him back again? I will go to him one day, but he cannot return to me."
(2 Samuel 12:16-23, NLT)

After seven days, the child died, and like flipping a switch, David moved on like nothing had happened - no time to grieve or reflect. Here again, we see the pattern of David compartmentalizing what he needed to deal with and just moving forward like nothing had ever happened.

Maybe with all this history, we can see how dysfunction operated in David's house. Shame, grief and anger were constantly being pushed down inside. And this is, unfortunately, a part of modern day culture, as well. Surely, we all know and love people who have found themselves in the depths of dysfunction and mistrust after having lived for years tied up in the secrets of their families, roped and gagged with the voices of people who loved and were tasked with protecting us, but instead met us with imperatives such as: *Just be quiet! It's over now; Let it go. Protect the family. Ignore it, and it will all go away.*

It is impossible for sons to feel safe and secure enough to be honest and transparent with a father who has buried his own shame and anger for generations. We cannot have a nurturing environment when we fail to protect our children, choosing, rather, to protect our images and our reputations. Healthy father – son relationships do not avoid pain by keeping silent. The need for heart-to-heart connections demands heart-to-heart communications without the fear of judgment or rejection.

I have walked through many of the victories and defeats of raising our two children, several nephews and nieces and a few other kids in our faith family. I have seen the transformation possible when you create a safe place of affirmation and accountability without shame or condemnation. I have also experienced the thrill of victory and the agony of defeat as we have pastored, counseled and mentored more people than I could begin to remember over the past thirty years.

One particular story comes to my mind when I think of the power of shame. I have a spiritual son who has a powerful gift to preach. We have walked together for many years, and I have watched him and his wife build and lead a powerful ministry in a difficult region of the world. The churches they have built and the communities they have impacted are remarkable. But a few years ago it became clear that not everything was healthy, and the signs of depression and burnout were obvious. The marriage and family life was suffering. The withdrawal and disconnection we experienced startled me. It was after several weeks of prayer and meditation that I felt strongly that I needed to do more than call or reach out. I knew that I needed to get on a plane and get face to face with my spiritual son and daughter. So, I planned the trip on a very short notice and went to spend several days with them - no preaching, no conference - just face-to-face, heart-to-heart, honest conversation. There were many laughs and tears and hopeful conversation; however, the moment we began to discuss shame, something began to happen that I cannot explain. When I talked about how shame traps you in a place of isolation and guilt, I knew the Holy Spirit was working deep inside at that moment.

There were days of fellowship and dialogue, but it was one conversation that changed everything. I had no idea what the impact would be and really was just recounting a conversation that I had recently had with my wife, Brenda. When she and I were talking about my trip to intervene, I made the statement that this young man was not like a son. *"He is my son,"* I said. I know that my natural son and daughter have a unique place in my heart and life, but that is not what I am comparing them to. I was stating that there is a huge difference in being like something versus being. The power of shame began to be broken, and healing began to happen at a deeper level.

"Shame loves secrecy. The most dangerous thing to do after a shaming experience is hide or bury our story. When we bury our story, the shame metastasizes. Shame is "I am

bad." Guilt is "I did something bad." Owning our story can be hard but not nearly as difficult as spending our lives running from it. Embracing our vulnerabilities is risky but not nearly as dangerous as giving up on love and belonging and joy–the experiences that make us the most vulnerable. Only when we are brave enough to explore the darkness will we discover the infinite power of our light."

- Brené Brown

Another spiritual son of mine encouraged me with a testimony about his evolution as a father and about what he learned in a time I taught him about fatherhood by not showing up:

When I think of my relationship with Bishop Marlon and what truly connected my heart to his, this is the first story that comes to mind. I was hosting a conference and had just begun going to church with Bishop Marlon and Pastor Brenda. (It was October 2003 and we had been attending their church since mid-August). We had several speakers lined up for the weekend and had invited other surrounding churches to join us as well. The Friday evening service came and went with no sign of the Williamson Family. Honestly, I felt a little upset - more like disappointed that they didn't support this event that I was hosting. When I told Bishop Marlon that I missed him on Friday, his response was simple. "It was Friday night." I knew immediately what he meant.

You see, Friday night in the south during the fall is all about high school football. His son was playing football,

*and his daughter was a cheerleader. It was Friday night,
and he never missed a game!*

*The disappointment I had felt turned to pride very quickly.
I had met a pastor who actually put his family first. I was
a young man in my mid-twenties, recently married, and
this one thing has formed my thought process my entire
marriage and continued on into being a parent. I am
the husband I am because of his influence on me as a
husband. I am the father I am because of his real-life
example as to what it looks like to be a dad. My relationship with Bishop Marlon has directly impacted the most
important thing in my life... my family. He taught me to
pay attention to first things.*

- Brian K. Wooten

It is amazing what we can teach when we have no idea we are
even teaching - just by modeling, just by being an example and
being willing to teach others by example. I am so glad Brian felt
close enough to me to mention that he missed me that night. If
he hadn't, who knows whether I would have thought to convey
my priorities. I am amazed when I see how God uses little things
like these to powerfully impact lives going forward. In the end,
that is what we all need, isn't it? Someone to show us the way.
This is why those of us who were abandoned and neglected so
often go into family life, feeling as if we are blindly groping in
the night, just trying to figure it out. And what a blessing when
God leads us to teach others in the midst of our own learning.
My son, Chad, shared this as a text message to my wife recently.
She shared, and I am sharing with his permission:

*Dad has always worked hard. I can remember when I was
old enough, probably not much older than my nine year
old son, he started taking me to work with him on Satur-
days or during school breaks. He found things for
me to do and made me feel helpful. Looking back and
knowing him, this was probably more trouble for him
than it was help, but I can still remember being excited to
go and feeling grown up. I was proud of him - of being the
boss's son. Now I catch myself working a lot, but I take my
son to work now and then. I can see my son is proud to
have me as a dad, and I know the feeling.*
- **Chad Williamson**

Something in me can't help but see the contrast in how Chad felt
about me and about himself when he shadowed me in those
early years with how I felt about my stepfather and about myself
as I learned from him. If we mapped the emotions on an
emotion wheel, they would come nowhere close to one another.
It strikes me that this is a good litmus test for us as fathers -
physical and spiritual fathers alike. Once the teaching is done,
how do our sons and daughters feel about us, and, more
importantly, how do they feel about themselves. The fruits of
hitting it right, when we do, are a palpable blessing. You can't
imagine my joy (or maybe you can) when I envision my
grandson, building his own sense of self and connection with
his father as they work and learn together. This is what it's
all about.

CHAPTER TEN
The Voice of a Father

There was a time in my life when church titles made me
uncomfortable, and I still have some discomfort with them,
if I'm honest. *Bishop* this and *prophet* this and apostle that and
doctor this left me with a feeling of discomfort that, I think,
came from an understanding that a title alone doesn't mean
someone has a function or that he is truly called or gifted or
even honest about what it is he is presenting himself to be.
What I do understand and value is this honorable principle
of recognizing, identifying, and receiving whoever people are
in whatever gift or office they may hold in the church, but
I understand that it has to come in order of function. When
I think about the voice of a father in any of our lives, I'm aware
of its powerful importance. I grew up in a home where there
was really no affirmation or no paternal affection. I can't
begrudge the man I called dad for this because he had no idea
how to give those things. It's a difficult thing to give what
you've never had. He did not know how to give affection
because he had never had it.

What developed in me was not victimhood. I didn't hold pity
parties for myself. On the contrary, what it bred in me was the
rebellious, *I-don't-need-you* persona of a self-driven young man,

intent on proving I didn't need a daddy, didn't need his support, and didn't need his voice. And, out of that, I was driven toward success, but it was always connected to performance. When we live in an orphan or servant mentality, we are driven toward success out of a need for affirmation. What I do recognize is that God always placed in my life teachers, coaches, and fathers of friends - adults who gave me affirmation that I desperately needed to hear. I later realized that I may have been drawn toward many of my closest friends because of how I saw their fathers relate to them in a way that I unconsciously desired for myself, and I can certainly see, in retrospect, that God was using others to speak over me the blessings that my heart desperately longed for.

The most important thing about the voice of a father in your life is that it can remove all doubt of who you are. Every day in your life, you will face voices that challenge who you really are. There is something divinely supernatural about what your father has spoken over you, and those words will come back to you in moments when your knees shake. What your father says of you is powerfully important. Jesus, Himself, experienced this.

> *And as Jesus rose up out of the water, the heavenly realm opened up over him and he saw the Holy Spirit descend out of the heavens and rest upon him in the form of a dove. Then suddenly the voice of the Father shouted from the sky, saying, "This is the Son I love, and my greatest delight is in him."* (**Mathew 3:16-17, TPT**)

By the time Jesus reached this stage in His life, it is safe to say that He surely knew who He was. The voice of affirmation did not come to make Him a son; it came to *affirm* that He was a son. And not only a son, but a son in whom His Father *delights*. If Jesus, being in perfect union with the Father, needed affirmation, then surely, we have the same need.

The voice from the Father to Jesus that day immediately preceded his forty days of testing in the wilderness. Clearly, this affirmation was profoundly important, not just for onlookers to hear, but for the ears of the Son. The affirming words of His father would shore him up against the tactics the enemy would use to assault Him in the coming days.

> *Then the tempter came to entice him to provide food by doing a miracle. So he said to Jesus, "How can you possibly be the Son of God and go hungry? Just order these stones to be turned into loaves of bread."*
> **(Matthew 4:3, TPT)**

> *"If you're really God's Son, jump, and the angels will catch you. For it is written in the Scriptures: He will command his angels to protect you and they will lift you up so that you won't even bruise your foot on a rock."*
> **(Matthew 4:6, TPT)**

The accuser went right to the heart of the identity issue. *If you are who the father said you are, prove it!* The challenge was not over miracle-working power or angelic protection. The test could be embodied in these questions: *Do you believe what the Father said about you? Why don't you use your power to save yourself? Why suffer if you are the son of God?*

And he didn't stop there. All the way to the cross, the same accuser raised the same question:

> *And one of the evil-doers who were hanged,*
> *was speaking evil of him, saying, 'If thou be*
> *the Christ, save thyself and us.'*
> **(Luke 23:39, YLT)**

From the day of His baptism, all the way to the last few hours on the cross, the enemy attacked the one thing that kept Him sure and steadfast in His purpose; He knew his identity was secure because he heard the voice of his Father say so. The voice of a father has the ability to remove all the insecurity and doubts about who we truly are, especially when we face suffering and hardship.

> *For he received from God the Father honour and glory,*
> *when there came such a voice to him from the excellent*
> *glory, This is my beloved Son, in whom I am well pleased.*
> **(2 Peter 1:17, KJV)**

Jesus received glory and honor *when the voice came.* When the voice of the Father speaks into your life, it empowers you in ways that will have a supernatural effect on your life. It's not always measurable. It's not always observable. Jesus was already everything he was going to be, but He still needed to hear the Father declare who He was.

From Genesis, we know without doubt that when God speaks, things happen. If God had not spoken over the abyss, would anything have changed? Notice that, after God finished creating, He blessed His creation. He blessed the creatures, animals, fish, birds, etc. He had just created them, and then, He blessed them, speaking over them that they should be fruitful and multiply. Creation brought them to the present. Blessing released them into their potential future, and both required words from the Father.

When God blessed the creation, He spoke over the future.

And again, after He created male and female, and afterwards, He blessed them. For years, I read and studied and preached this passage and did not understand that this was a blessing. When God spoke the blessing over Adam and Eve, He was saying: *This is what I want for your future.* Be fruitful. Multiply. Replenish. Subdue. Have dominion. This was more than a mandate; this was a blessing. It was God speaking *success* over humankind - not to just perform, but to, under the authority of God, be fruitful, multiply, and have dominion over the earth.

> *And God blessed them, saying, Be fruitful, and*
> *multiply, and fill the waters in the seas, and let*
> *fowl multiply in the earth.*
> **(Genesis 1:22, KJV)**

> *And God blessed them, and God said unto them,*
> *Be fruitful, and multiply, and replenish the earth, and*
> *subdue it: and have dominion over the fish of the sea, and*
> *over the fowl of the air, and over every living thing that*
> *moveth upon the earth.* **(Genesis 1:28, KJV)**

Creation is brand new, and man has just arrived; what could be missing? Apparently, in the mind of God, there was something more needed; a blessing. *Be fruitful!* The voice of a father's blessing releases potential. In this case, God was unlocking the future that was already in creation. God was not demanding something; He was blessing and releasing it.

This is ultimately what the voice of the father is supposed to do in our lives. It is to affirm us, to equip us, and to empower us. At the end of the day, it is to be a voice that says, "I am speaking to your future."

When we position and align ourselves properly with the leaders who God has gifted to us, they have the power to speak into our lives and to release glory and honor. Honor is voice-activated. Because we are created in the image and likeness of God, we possess the power to create with our spoken words.

> *"The Holy Spirit is the one who gives life, that which is of the natural realm is of no help. The words I speak to you are Spirit and life. But there are still some of you who won't believe."* **(John 6:63, TPT)**

Notice that the scripture did not say the words that were written or thought, but the words that were spoken. The words that are spoken are *spirit* and *life*. We have all heard the old saying, "sticks and stones may break my bones, but words will never hurt me." This is a cute comeback, but anyone over the age of three knows that it is absolutely false. In fact, I'm convinced that most of the broken hearts and lives in our world are the result of words.

I yearn to come and be face-to-face with you and get to
know you. For I long to impart to you the gift of the Spirit
that will empower you to stand strong in your faith. Now,
this means that when we come together and are side by
side, something wonderful will be released. We can expect
to be co-encouraged and co-comforted by each other's faith!
(Romans 1:11-12, TPT)

Notice, the Apostle Paul says that there is something that we experience only in face-to-face meetings. It is not possible to get the impartation of a father by simply reading or studying his writing. You cannot get it from social media. The power and authority of a father to bless a son is phenomenal. I see so many folks struggling and wrestling to be successful in life and in ministry. Yet so many of them are attempting to go it alone. They never know the power of being blessed by the voice of a father. There is a pattern all through the scripture as to how blessing is released, and it is evident from the very beginning:

And the Lord spake unto Moses, saying, Speak unto
Aaron and unto his sons, saying, On this wise ye shall
bless the children of Israel, saying unto them, The Lord
bless thee, and keep thee: The Lord make his face shine
upon thee, and be gracious unto thee: The Lord lift up his
countenance upon thee, and give thee peace. And they
shall put my name upon the children of Israel; and I will
bless them. **(Numbers 6:22-27, KJV)**

Wow! Moses and Aaron release *"God's blessing"* on the children of Israel by simply saying what God said over them. The words we speak are spirit and life. *The power of life and death are in our tongues.* Our very salvation is connected to the heart believing and the mouth confessing. We see this repeated over and over with Noah, Abraham, Isaac, Jacob and his sons. As I have already stated, first and last things are weighty matters. Consider the last thing Jesus did before he ascended following his resurrection:

> *Then Jesus led them to Bethany, and lifting his hands to heaven, he blessed them. While he was blessing them, he left them and was taken up to heaven.* (**Luke 24:50-51, NLT**)

Just as Jesus was about to ascend out of sight, his final act was to speak blessings over the men he had just spent more than three years teaching and training. You see, even our best teaching must be accompanied with our blessing.

I don't know how many readers might follow Frank Caprio. He is a judge, whose courtroom is televised, and who is known for being both fair and compassionate to those who find themselves before him, usually for traffic violations and other minor alleged infractions. In a recent interview, he shared a memory that brought him to tears. At the end of his sixth-grade year, his classmates had autograph books that they had each other sign, and the judge said he didn't know why he did it, but he came home with his book and asked his dad to sign it. In this interview, this man, well into his eighties, tears in his eyes, emotion welling in his voice, noted the extended time his dad spent choosing his words, and then he quoted, *word-for-word*, the message his father had written to and for him more than seventy years before:

*The road is long, the road is hard and very bumpy, but
I know that you will proceed with honor and dignity to
the end of the highest learning.
From your dad, Antonio Caprio Sr.*

These words became an umbrella over the future judge's life.
At the time, their family had very little. They were living in a
cold-water flat, his family having just the necessities of life. But
the judge explains why this made his father's words all the more
powerful for him. "This was a dream for my father; this was a
path he was trying to give me in life." (**Caprio 2024**)

The heart's cry of a spiritual father is one that says, I want you to
have everything I've got, and I won't be jealous or intimidated
if you have more. In fact, my greatest success will be when you
have more.

I personally know the power of being blessed by the voice of a
father. I love the teaching and revelation that comes from many
great men and women of God. But, when you experience the
empowerment that only comes from the voice of a father, you
know the difference between a great teacher and a true father.
When a son knows that his father believes in him, he has the
courage and confidence to withstand even the most challenging
of circumstances.

If you want to bless your children, you are going to have to say
some things to them about them. Thank God for prayers. It is
appropriate and needful that we go into our closets and pray
for our children, but there is nothing more powerful than what

your child hears you say about him or her. There is nothing more powerful to your children's future than that they hear your voice declare who they are and what their future is about. That is how we bless our children.

There are things you can prophesy for yourself, speak over yourself, believe for yourself, decree for yourself, and accomplish by yourself, and those things are wonderful. But there are some things you will never walk in and never experience until someone with greater authority declares and decrees and releases something into your life. The spiritual dynamics of the voice of the Father speaking over your life will unleash blessings you can't speak for yourself.

Romans 1:11 reads: "For I long to see you, that I may impart unto you some spiritual gift, to the end ye may be established."

Paul had something for them that he couldn't send by messenger, that they couldn't read in a letter, that he could not impart unless they were face-to-face. I believe there is a blessing that God delivers in our lives when we receive the voice of the father through the spiritual fathers and mentors he places in our lives. I can tell you this because I have walked it out, and I have seen it as a spiritual son and as a spiritual father. When we start to realize that God has sent spiritual leaders to be the voice of the father to us, we understand that we gather together for more than the sermon of the week. There are things that happen in the presence of one another that do not happen any other way.

CHAPTER ELEVEN

Spiritual Covering

*Obey them that have the rule over you and submit
yourselves: for they watch for your souls, as they must
give account, that they may do it with joy, and not with
grief: for that is unprofitable for you.*
(Hebrews 13:17, KJV)

As we shift our paradigm to a kingdom mandate, one of the
major issues we often struggle with has to do with the fact that
a kingdom does not function like a democracy. The majority
does not rule in a kingdom. The word of the king is the ultimate
and final authority. This is especially a struggle in our American
culture. We pride ourselves on our independence and self-
determination. We are proud to be American and *free*. Contrary
to much of the pop culture of today, the truth is that freedom
must be held in a healthy tension with responsibility and
accountability. We are free to do almost anything we choose,
but we are not free to choose the consequences of those choices.

Over my years of ministry and teaching about the value of
covenant relationships and spiritual fathers, I have often been
challenged to give biblical support for the concept of spiritual
covering. I have specifically been told that it is not in the Bible,

to which I respond that there are many new covenant truths and principles that are not necessarily stated in exact words, but nevertheless, are found in principle within the scriptures.

I am aware that there have been abuses and extremes in this area of understanding. But just as every counterfeit is worthless, the counterfeit is also based on something real and true. There was an original that had real value, or the counterfeit would not have been made. No one makes counterfeit pennies. We cannot abandon the truth when it is misused; we must search for the hidden original and hold it forth in plain sight.

One of the misconceptions of spiritual covering is that we use this excuse to hide people's sins and failures. I see covering more like a covering of a wound or injury. It is not to hide it, but to heal it and to prevent infection from spreading to others close by.

What can we find in the scripture to support the concept of spiritual covering? Hebrews 13:17 is a good place to start. The word *covering* is not in the text, but the idea is obvious: "Obey them that have the rule over you and submit yourselves..."

We are commanded to obey and submit to those that God has given to "rule over" us. It is clear that there are those who God has ordained to be in places of authority in our lives. In order for us to walk this out, we must come under what is over us. This sounds like a covering to me. If I am under a blanket or under a tent, then I am covered. If I am under the authority of the leadership God has ordained in my life, I am under their covering. This is not some hierarchy or denominational pattern. This is a new covenant kingdom order. There are powerful blessings found when we come into alignment and order according to God's pattern.

> *A Song of degrees of David. Behold, how good and how*
> *pleasant it is for brethren to dwell together in unity! It is*
> *like the precious ointment upon the head, that ran down*
> *upon the beard, even Aaron's beard: that went down to the*
> *skirts of his garments; As the dew of Hermon, and as the*
> *dew that descended upon the mountains of Zion: for there*
> *the LORD commanded the blessing, even life for evermore.*
> **(Psalm 133:1-3, KJV)**

The picture we see in the scripture is two-fold. The first is the oil running down from Aaron's head all the way to the hem of his garments. The second is the dew that descends from the top of Mt. Hermon and finally flows through Palestine as the Jordan River. According to the Strong's Hebrew Dictionary, the name Jordan means to *descend*.

Physically, Hermon was to Canaan what Aaron was ceremonially to Israel—its head and crown, from which the fertilizing stores of heaven descended over the land. For not only does the one great river of Palestine, the Jordan, issue from the roots of Hermon, but the giant mountain is constantly gathering and sending off clouds, which float down even to Southern Zion.

The real subject of this passage is unity and harmony. To dwell together in this original language was to have a covenant language. It meant to settle together. It can even be seen as meaning *to marry one another.* The end result is that there is a place where the commanded blessing of God is released like the flowing of the Jordan River in our lives.

We must not miss the repeated principle mentioned in the text. The oil and the dew descended from a head. We must see that the concept of covering is likened to having a headship over our lives. The beauty is that the same anointing and blessing that is on the head flows down to the body. When we align ourselves properly in harmony where God places us in the Body, the flow of His blessings will bring life and fruitfulness!

Proper alignment is vital when we consider joining ourselves together. If you remain isolated and independent, alignment is unnecessary. But when we connect and join our hearts together, it is critical that we find our place. It is in this grace we will experience supernatural blessing and favor. It is here that we have protection and provision.

> *But let all who take refuge in you rejoice; let them sing joyful praises forever. Spread your protection over them, that all who love your name may be filled with joy. For you bless the godly, O LORD; you surround them with your shield of love.* (**Psalm 5:11 -12, NLT**)

What does this look like? How does God surround us with a shield of love? How does He spread His protection over us? How does He cover us? I believe that this occurs when we come under the covering of Godly leadership and covenant relationships with the rest of the body. We cannot just experience love all alone or just between God and ourselves. It has to be experienced in fellowship and harmony with our family and the church. We cannot simply say that we submit to God, and He is our covering. To do so is to violate the principles of honor and submission.

The pattern throughout the scripture reveals that God has always provided a father – son covering:

- Adam and Eve discovered that they were naked (un-covered) after they took the forbidden fruit. The un-covering had nothing to do with clothing; it couldn't have because they had no clothes before. When they disobeyed and rebelled, the glory and protection was lifted. The son became disconnected from his father. The shame and guilt of a sin conscience was the result. **(Genesis 3:1-11)**

- The anointing that came on the priesthood was passed down from Aaron to his sons in his oil-soaked garments. **(Leviticus 8:1-13)**

- The favor of Jacob was on Joseph and seen in the coat of many colors. This was the first thing stripped from him when he was falsely accused and thrown in prison. **(Genesis 37:23)**

- The mantle of Elijah was passed to his spiritual son Elisha when he was caught up with the chariots of fire. **(2 Kings 2:1-14)**

- The prodigal son was clothed with the best robe in the house when he returned. I submit that the best robe in the house belonged to the father.
  (Luke 15:22-24)

All of these examples show the pattern of spiritual covering.

Another pattern we see all through the scripture is that the believers are referred to as sheep. I am not sure this is a compliment, but one thing for sure is that no sheep is safe in this world without a good shepherd.

Feed the flock of God which is among you, taking the oversight thereof, not by constraint, but willingly; not for filthy lucre, but of a ready mind; Neither as being lords over God's heritage, but being ensamples to the flock.
(1 Peter 5:2-3, KJV)

As a follower of Christ, we are given Godly examples to follow and to submit to. These elders and shepherds watch over us. It stands to reason that if these leaders are set over us, then we are set under their covering. The challenge to those of us who are called to lead is to be a model for the flock, rather than seeing ourselves as lords. Jesus was both the Son and the good shepherd.

As the Father knoweth me, even so know I the Father: and I lay down my life for the sheep. **(John 10:15, KJV)**

When we begin to model this relationship properly, we will be living the most attractive life imaginable. When leaders know the Father, and the sheep see a shepherd willing to lay down his life - his agenda, his control and his comfort - on their behalf, submitting to authority will not be an issue. It will not be about control or being under someone's thumb. It will produce life and freedom on an entirely new level. It will establish our hearts with confidence and with the assurance of favor and grace.

And we beseech you, brethren, to know them which labour among you, and are over you in the Lord, and admonish you; And to esteem them very highly in love for their work's sake. And be at peace among yourselves.
(1 Thessalonians 5:12-13, KJV)

To highly esteem those over you means to give them the greatest respect, honor and value. It means to offer them great admiration and appreciation. These qualities require us to give proper place to those God has given to us. When these qualities are working in us, great blessings flow to us.

CHAPTER TWELVE

Generational Inheritance

"A good man leaves an inheritance
to his children's children."
(Proverbs 13:22, KJV)

It is no coincidence that the New Testament opens with a long list of names, establishing the lineage of Jesus all the way back to Abraham. We often skim over these portions of scripture. These long lists of names reveal to us the importance of this valuable truth - that God has *always* been a multi-generational God. He has always been planning a family lineage. This lineage is only possible through the father – son heritage. Remember, slaves, servants and orphans did not receive an inheritance.

In my early years as a Christian, numerous bad seeds were planted in my thinking. One of the earliest was the idea that my greatest hope in life was to eventually die or to get raptured so I could go to my heavenly inheritance. The problem with this thought, though, lies in the fact that we receive an inheritance when someone else dies, not when we die. Once I began to understand that the Father was offering me an inheritance in *this life*, now, my world view had to change.

God's plan all along has been to fill the earth with His sons, and they are to be fruitful and increase. As sons, we are to reflect His image and to carry His heart to the world. This is why we pray "Thy Kingdom come, on earth as it is in heaven."

> *The Lord shall increase you more and more, you and your*
> *children. Ye are blessed of the Lord which made heaven*
> *and earth. The heaven, even the heavens, are the Lord's:*
> *but the earth hath he given to the children of men.*
> **(Psalm 115:14-16, KJV)**

> *Blessed are the meek: for they shall inherit the earth.*
> **(Matthew 5:5, KJV)**

The Lord made heaven and earth, but this scripture declares a powerful and much ignored truth; the earth has been given to the children of men. Once I became aware of my Kingdom inheritance, I realized that God was always in the all-knowing position of authority, but He was not always in control. He has never withdrawn the dominion given to man in the garden over creation. In fact, once I saw this, I understood why there is so much out of order in our world today. I am not saying that God cannot or will not get involved and intervene in our world, but He will only do it in partnership with our participation, prayers and through His relationship with His sons.

> *So you have not received a spirit that makes you fearful*
> *slaves. Instead, you received God's Spirit when he adopted*
> *you as his own children. Now we call him, "Abba, Father."*
> *For his Spirit joins with our spirit to affirm that we are*

God's children. And since we are his children, we are his
heirs. In fact, together with Christ we are heirs of God's
glory. But if we are to share his glory, we must also share
his suffering. (**Romans 8:15-17, TPT**)

We often forget to keep the scriptures in context when we read
them. It is critical that we understand the audience and the
culture at the time the author is writing. In Hebrew culture,
inheritance was a huge deal. In fact, only sons were qualified to
receive an inheritance. This is why in the new covenant, even
the female is considered a son; there is no male or female in
Christ. We are His heirs! We share in all that is His, including
His glory and His suffering. We are His offspring and share in
His divine nature.

For you are all children of God through faith in Christ
Jesus. And all who have been united with Christ in
baptism have put on Christ, like putting on new clothes.
There is no longer Jew or Gentile, slave or free, male and
female. For you are all one in Christ Jesus.
(**Galatians 3:26-28, NLT**)

As we have already stated, Elisha wanted the double portion
blessing from Elijah. He did not want his mantle or ministry;
he wanted sonship. Why? Because if you are a son, especially
the firstborn, the inheritance will come, but sonship must be
established first.

We also saw that the younger son in Luke 15 failed to see
the true value of the father – son relationship and got the

inheritance but lost his identity. He was living in an ocean of plenty, and he asked for a bucket-full and left.

Just like the war that is happening over the seed, there is also a strategy designed to disrupt the generational blessings that flow through spiritual inheritance. In the kingdom of God, there is always divine order. The order of inheritance is directly connected to sonship.

I often see stories in the scripture and react with the thought, *Wow, that was tough!* One of these was the story of how Esau lost his inheritance:

Esau said to Jacob, "I'm starved! Give me some of that red stew!" (This is how Esau got his other name, Edom, which means "red.") "All right," Jacob replied, "but trade me your rights as the firstborn son." "Look, I'm dying of starvation!" said Esau. "What good is my birthright to me now?" **(Genesis 25:30-32, NLT)**

As I have continued my journey in the father – son life, it has become clearer and clearer to me that what Esau did was much more devastating than what many would consider a big deal. We see men of God commit adultery or get tangled up in some other scandal and quickly disqualify them. However, Esau gave up the most precious thing a son could possess, and he traded it for a single bowl of stew. He dishonored and devalued his father's heritage. He stepped out of divine order and derailed his entire future and his sons' just to satisfy a momentary craving.

We see this in the wickedness of Ahab and Jezebel. In this

story, we find that Ahab has set his sights on a certain vineyard, and he offered what seemed to be a good price to Naboth, the owner, but he failed to understand the importance of the land to Naboth, because Naboth knew how to value the land as an inheritance:

> *And Ahab spake unto Naboth, saying, Give me thy vineyard, that I may have it for a garden of herbs, because it is near unto my house: and I will give thee for it a better vineyard than it; or, if it seem good to thee, I will give thee the worth of it in money. And Naboth said to Ahab, The Lord forbid it me, that I should give the inheritance of my fathers unto thee.* (**1 Kings 21:2-3, KJV**)

Ahab wanted a vineyard, but Naboth did not own a vineyard; he owned an inheritance. Unlike a vegetable garden, which can be planted in one place this year and another place next year, a vineyard is a long-term proposition. It takes years for vines to grow sturdy enough to produce grapes, and it takes careful nurture to get good grapes. The land he possessed was more than property; it was not about the appraisal value. In fact, Ahab was offering him a better piece of land. For Ahab, this was a simple monetary transaction—the purchase of something that had caught his eye. For Naboth, his vineyard was more important than money—this was a family heritage, a sacred trust.

Jezebel then got involved. She came in and found King Ahab sulking, discouraged and sad over the situation. She asked him, "Are you not the king?" We don't need to gloss over the intent behind her words. She was criticizing and actually disrespecting the king. Just like the Jezebel spirit always does, she set out to get what she wanted at all costs.

Jezebel assumed the king's authority, wrote letters in his name, signed them with his seal, the sign of the king's authority, and tasked the elders and nobles of the city to carry out her bidding. These officials would be hard-pressed to refuse Jezebel. They knew the power that she wielded, and they knew her lack of scruples. If they had refused to do her bidding, they might have been next in line for execution.

Rather than deal with Naboth directly, Jezebel devised a scheme to insulate Ahab from blame. The officials that she tasked to conduct the fast are to locate two unscrupulous men who will bring false witness against Naboth, accusing him of cursing God (blasphemy), and cursing the king (treason).

The men of his city, even the elders and the nobles who lived in his city, did as Jezebel had sent to them, according as it was written in the letters which she had sent to them. The city officials, either to curry Ahab's favor or to avoid Jezebel's disfavor, carried out Jezebel's plot and murdered Naboth.

> *"It happened, when Jezebel heard that Naboth was stoned,*
> *and was dead, that Jezebel said to Ahab, Arise, take*
> *possession of the vineyard of Naboth the Jezreelite,*
> *which he refused to give you for money; for Naboth is*
> *not alive, but dead."* (**1 Kings 21:15, WEB**)

Even though Naboth was dead, his land would not automatically go to the King. However, 2 Kings 9:26 suggests that Jezebel had Naboth's sons killed as well, so that they could not inherit the land. No sooner than Ahab took possession of Naboth's inheritance, the word of the Lord came to Elijah:

King Ahab of Israel is in Naboth's vineyard right now, taking it over. Go tell him that I say, 'Ahab, you murdered Naboth and took his property. And so, in the very spot where dogs licked up Naboth's blood, they will lick up your blood.'

> *When Elijah found him, Ahab said, "So, my enemy, you found me at last." Elijah answered: Yes, I did! Ahab, you have managed to do everything the Lord hates. Now you will be punished. You and every man and boy in your family will die, whether slave or free. Your whole family will be wiped out, just like the families of King Jeroboam and King Baasha. You've made the LORD very angry by sinning and causing the Israelites to sin. And as for Jezebel, dogs will eat her body there in Jezreel.*
> (1 King 21:18-23, CEV)

God responded to the corruption and deception of Ahab and Jezebel, and He communicated through Elijah. It is important to note that this whole situation was all about a son's inheritance. This was never about a piece of land. The judgment of God was devastating not only to Ahab, but also his entire lineage, possibly because Ahab and Jezebel did not just murder one man and take one vineyard; they destroyed the lineage of Naboth.

Ahab and Jezebel failed to see that Naboth was not a slave

or servant; he was a son. What the king wanted could not be bought or bartered for. Naboth knew the vineyard was his inheritance.

> *And slaves don't stay in the family forever*
> *though the Son will always remain in the family.*
> **(John 8:35, CEV)**

Jesus said that sons are members of the family, but servants are not. From the beginning, God wanted offspring who would relate to Him in love, not slaves or hired hands who would obey Him out of obligation. Servants may relate to their master on a superficial level, but no intimacy or sense of family exists. Sons, on the other hand, are part of the family; they are heirs who will inherit everything that belongs to their father. What an empowering revelation when we finally come to see who we truly are:

- *We are the children of the Kingdom!*
- *We are His offspring!*
- *We have the divine nature of our heavenly Father!*
- *We are joint and equal heirs with Jesus!*

> *Jesus left the crowds and went inside the house where he was staying. Then his disciples approached him and asked, "Please explain the deeper meaning of the parable of the weeds growing in the field of wheat." He answered, "The man who sowed his field with good seed represents me, the Son of Man. And the field is the world. The good seeds I sow are the children of the kingdom…*(**Matthew 13:36-38, TPT**)

We are the harvest of sons the Father reaped by sowing His only begotten son in the earth. Now, we must rise up and take possession of our inheritance as sons of God. We must allow the spiritual fathers in our lives to circumcise our hearts and bring maturity so that we can be responsible heirs. We need our orphan hearts healed so we can be confident and stable in the Father's house.

So, what exactly is it that we inherit in this new covenant? What does it look like?

> *So, don't ever be afraid, dearest friends! Your loving Father joyously gives you his kingdom realm with all its promises!* **(Luke 12:32, TPT)**

> *What a wonderful thought that the Father is full of joy - that it brings Him great pleasure to give us His kingdom. It gives a king great pleasure to give what is sovereignly his to his progeny. This could be why the scripture says, "For the joy set before him, Jesus endured the cross."*
> **(Hebrews 12:2, KJV)**

> *You have stayed with me in all my troubles. So I will give you the right to rule as kings, just as my Father has given me the right to rule as a king.* **(Luke 22:28-29, CEV)**

Jesus was telling the faithful followers that because they remained with him through the suffering, they would now follow Him to the place of kingdom authority. We can now reign in this life through our lives in Christ. We no longer live as slaves or vagabonds, wandering aimlessly through this life. We are overcomers because He overcame.

> *To him that overcometh will I grant to sit with me in my throne, even as I also overcame, and am set down with my Father in his throne.* (**Revelation 3:21, KJV**)

I have preached the gospel of the Kingdom for over thirty years now. I cannot count the times that I have witnessed the moment when the light comes, and someone sees who they are in the Father's Kingdom. The message of kingdom inheritance is the answer to every dilemma in every nation of the world. In fact, every human has a built-in desire to rule over their world, not over people, but over their circumstances and future. This is our inheritance.

> *This desire to be free to pursue one's personal dreams and to maximize one's potential is the foundation of the democratic ideal and is embraced as the ultimate standard of a free society. However, the societies and communities that have tried this noble "freedom" experiment are still plagued with the inconsistencies of inequality, racism, prejudice, injustice, corruption, jealousy, suspicion, competition, abuse, neglect, and a clear disparity between the "haves" and "have-nots." In the end, mankind has become imprisoned by his pursuit of freedom.*
> (**Rediscovering the Kingdom, M. Munroe, 138**)

I have come to the conclusion that the common pursuit of all humans is the pursuit of power and the desire to possess the ability to control one's circumstances and destiny. When I use the term power, I am not referring to the tyrannical, oppressive, dictatorial control of people, but rather the ability to control one's own circumstances and environment. It is this lack of control over our daily lives, situations, and circumstances that makes us feel so helpless and live as victims of life. For many of us, life is simply a daily struggle as we try to stay afloat in a sea of uncertainty and pressures of all sorts. At the same time, we wrestle with a sense of dignified slavery to the institutions of our societies.

> *Our desire and passion to gain this power to control our circumstances and environment is the motivation for our behavior. We strive to gain positions of influence in order to accumulate financial wealth. We seek the power that money promises us: political and spiritual power, the accumulation of status symbols, superior knowledge, and many other forms of controlling dispositions. I believe this pursuit for power is simply the pursuit of dominion over life.*
> **(Rediscovering the Kingdom, M. Munroe, 182)**

> *This is what the Sovereign LORD says: If the prince gives a gift of land to one of his sons as his inheritance, it will belong to him and his descendants forever. But if the prince gives a gift of land from his inheritance to one of his servants, the servant may keep it only until the Year of Jubilee, which comes every fiftieth year. At that time the land will return to the prince. But when the prince gives gifts to his sons, those gifts will be permanent.*
> **(Ezekiel 46:16-17, NLT)**

It is a beautiful thing that the Father has done in bringing us into His family as sons. Under the old covenant, a servant only had temporary possession of the land if they were fortunate enough to have a benevolent prince. We, on the other hand, have been given the full rights of inheritance in Christ. Too many of us are like the two sons in Luke 15 - some filled with guilt and shame from our time in the pig pen asking only to be a servant, and others preoccupied with working for the Father and never knowing that all He has is ours as well.

The book of Ruth conveys one of the most beautiful stories of restoration of inheritance:

> *Now it came to pass in the days when the judges ruled, that there was a famine in the land. And a certain man of Bethlehem-judah went to sojourn in the country of Moab, he, and his wife, and his two sons. And the name of the man was Elimelech, and the name of his wife Naomi, and the name of his two sons Mahlon and Chilion, Ephrathites of Bethlehem-Judah. And they came into the country of Moab, and continued there. And Elimelech Naomi's husband died; and she was left, and her two sons. And they took them wives of the women of Moab; the name of the one was Orpah, and the name of the other Ruth: and they dwelled there about ten years. And Mahlon and Chilion died also both of them; and the woman was left of her two sons and her husband.* (**Ruth 1:1-5, KJV**)

When we see the word, now, at the beginning of a story or passage, we should take a moment to see what preceded the story. The previous text says:

*In those days there was no king in Israel: every man did
that which was right in his own eyes.*
(Judges 21:25, KJV)

The setting and context here is that Israel had no king, and the
people went about doing what was right in their own sight. It is
no wonder that a famine was coming upon the land. Elimelech
and Naomi took their family and left Bethlehem-Judah (the
house of bread and praise) and dwelt in Moab for ten years. The
two sons married women from Moab, and in a short time, the
father and both sons died. In her bitterness and grief, Naomi
compelled her two daughters-in-law to return to their families.

It is interesting that neither of Naomi's sons had any children.
Whenever our lives are out of order, the real famine is not in
the land, but on the inside, and barrenness is usually the result.
So all that remained were Ruth and her two daughters-in-law,
widowed and grieving. Naomi told them that she had no sons
to offer them and no inheritance to provide for their futures.
She was crushed and empty. Orpah left without even saying
goodbye, but Ruth had a covenant heart and made a profound
statement:

*And Ruth said, Intreat me not to leave thee, or to return
from following after thee: for whither thou goest, I will go;
and where thou lodgest, I will lodge: thy people shall be
my people, and thy God my God: Where thou diest, will I
die, and there will I be buried: the LORD do so to me, and
more also, if ought but death part thee and me.*
(Ruth 1:16-17, KJV)

Naomi and Ruth returned to Bethlehem-Judah, and it was harvest time. The famine was over. The most beautiful part of the story unfolds with Ruth, out gleaning from the fields. She was getting enough to get by, but she caught the eye of Boaz, who owned the field. Boaz just happened to be a kinsman of Naomi. Eventually, Boaz went to the city gates and redeemed Naomi, her land and Ruth. The first order of business was a marriage. Boaz took Ruth, the Moabite, to be his wife.

> *So Boaz took Ruth, and she was his wife: and when he went in unto her, the LORD gave her conception, and she bare a son.* (**Ruth 4:13, KJV**)

What a beautiful picture of redemption! Ruth was no longer living as a foreign slave, struggling to get by. She not only found love and acceptance, but she has also come into an inheritance that she could have never dreamed possible. And not only did she get the harvest, but she also got the Lord of the harvest. And then, to top it all off, she produced a son. At last, their house was in order, a son was born, and the inheritance was secure.

We have the awesome privilege of being sons in the household of faith. Our heavenly father has joyfully given us His kingdom. Jesus, our heavenly brother, has given us the keys of this Kingdom. And now, we have the heaven on earth mandate to bring into our experience the father – son order that releases the blessings of this beautiful relationship. Fathers leave an inheritance to their children's children. We have been called to this father – son journey for the sake of our posterity, not for our own prosperity.

CHAPTER THIRTEEN

The War Over the Seed

We know that the sin problem entered the world in the garden with Adam's fall, but there is an interesting truth found in what God said to the serpent after the confrontation and blame game played out for us all to see.

> *And the LORD God said unto the serpent, Because thou hast done this, thou art cursed above all cattle, and above every beast of the field; upon thy belly shalt thou go, and dust shalt thou eat all the days of thy life: And I will put enmity between thee and the woman, and between thy seed and her seed; it shall bruise thy head, and thou shalt bruise his heel.* **(Genesis 3:14-15, KJV)**

Notice that God's plan for restoration and reconciliation was directly connected to a seed. We know ultimately that the promised seed was to Jesus the Messiah. Don't overlook the fact that the lineage and destiny of the seed was still connected to the woman. God did not have a plan to start over with a new seed. The seed was there when God spoke. To be more specific, the seed would come through generations of sons.

The serpent did not miss this. According to the Strong's Hebrew

Dictionary, the word enmity means to hate or to be hostile towards something. There was a spiritual war that began that day between evil and the future seed. We see it clearly in Exodus when Israel was in captivity and Pharaoh became concerned that the chosen people of God were multiplying in Egypt. They were put under extra heavy burdens and labor; however, the more they were afflicted, the more they increased.

> *And Pharaoh charged all his people, saying, every son that is born ye shall cast into the river, and every daughter ye shall save alive.* (**Exodus 1:22, KJV**)

The King of Egypt was under the spell of the evil one and made the decree for the midwives to cast every son in the river! The war was over the future, and the future was locked up in birthing sons. The exact same spirit of abortion was at work at the time Jesus was born.

> *After the wise men were gone, an angel of the Lord appeared to Joseph in a dream. "Get up! Flee to Egypt with the child and his mother," the angel said. "Stay there until I tell you to return, because Herod is going to search for the child to kill him." That night Joseph left for Egypt with the child and Mary, his mother, and they stayed there until Herod's death. This fulfilled what the Lord had spoken through the prophet: "I called my Son out of Egypt." Herod was furious when he realized that the wise men had outwitted him. He sent soldiers to kill all the boys in and around Bethlehem who were two years old and under, based on the wise men's report of the star's first appearance.* (**Matthew 2:13-16, NLT**)

As we look around our society and see the undeniable impact of the dysfunction of fatherless homes, we should recognize that the real war is still over our seed – our sons and daughters. When we see much of the same dysfunction in the church, we must confront this spiritual war over the spiritual household of faith as well.

There is no way to address the abortion issue in this writing, but I cannot talk about the war over the seed and not go there.

> *Approximately 862,320 abortions were performed in 2017, down 7% from 926,190 in 2014. The abortion rate in 2017 was 13.5 abortions per 1,000 women aged 15–44, down 8% from 14.6 per 1,000 in 2014. This is the lowest rate ever observed in the United States; in 1973, the year abortion became legal, the rate was 16.3.*
> **(Guttmacher, 2017)**

Moses wrote, "you shall not give any of your children to offer them to Molech, and so profane the name of your God: I am the Lord." **(Leviticus 18:21; cf. 20:2–5; Deuteronomy 18:10)**

In ancient Israel, Molech was the pagan god that promised fertile fields. While the scripture regularly extols the blessedness of children **(Psalm 127–28)**, in our country, many treat them as inconveniences to prosperity and hindrances to sexual liberation.

> *"Thou didst form my inward parts, thou didst knit me together in my mother's womb."* **(Psalm 139:13, RSV)**

Abortion is not merely a medical procedure that ends the life of a fetus inside the mother's womb in order to prevent the birth. Abortion is an ethical issue concerning what is right and what is wrong, what is good and what is evil, what is beautiful and what is grossly horrible, what is life and what is murder.

Those in favor of abortion cite a number of reasons for holding to their pro-choice positions. Some of these reasons eloquently defend the rights of the mother while others twist facts and statistics. When, however, the smoke screens are removed, the sad fact is that the vast majority of abortions performed in this country are done for social reasons. Rape, incest, life of the mother, and severe fetal deformity account for only 2-5 percent of all abortions. The remaining 95-98 percent are done strictly as a matter of convenience. According to the Alan Guttmacher Institute (formerly an affiliate of Planned Parenthood, the nation's largest abortion provider), more than 90 percent of the women seeking abortions are motivated primarily by the difficulty pregnancy would cause for their careers, education, finances, or family lives.

> *The prophet Jeremiah wrote of God's Words to him, "I chose you before I formed you in the womb; I set you apart before you were born."* **(Jeremiah 1:5, NLT)**

> *To the prophet Isaiah, God said, "And now, says the LORD, who formed me from the womb to be His servant"* **(Isaiah 49:5, NLT)**

Scripture reveals what it has taken science centuries to prove. The unborn fetus is not a blob, a mass of tissue similar to an egg yolk. The unborn fetus is a person who is developing. That living being within the mother's womb sleeps, kicks, and even sucks its thumb.

I have already mentioned the significance of Malachi 4:5-6, as it relates to the turning of hearts for fathers and sons, but there is also another truth seen in the prophecy:

> *Behold, I will send you Elijah the prophet before the coming of the great and dreadful day of the LORD: And he shall turn the heart of the fathers to the children, and the heart of the children to their fathers, lest I come and smite the earth with a curse.* (**Malachi 4:5-6, KJV**)

I have often pondered why God chose Elijah as the spirit or the anointing that would bridge the gap from the closing of the Old Testament and the opening of the new. I have several ideas including the obvious one we have seen in the father-son succession with Elisha. One dimension of this choice can also be seen in the conflict between Elijah and Jezebel. No other person in the scripture personifies the hostility and hatred of the seed more than Queen Jezebel. The idolatry of the Egyptian and Canaanite cultures had deep roots in the Hebrew people. Often this idolatry included sexual perversion and child sacrifice.

Jezebel was the daughter of a Phoenecian priest who was also a king who performed the regular service of sacrificing "children to Molech" as he served in the temple of Baal. This is not only Jezebel's bloodline, but she and Ahab enjoyed carrying out the sacrifices of children, *even their own*, as they led the Israelites in Baal worship.

But Ahab son of Omri did what was evil in the LORD's
sight, even more than any of the kings before him. And
as though it were not enough to follow the sinful example
of Jeroboam, he married Jezebel, the daughter of King
Ethbaal of the Sidonians, and he began to bow down in
worship of Baal. First Ahab built a temple and an altar for
Baal in Samaria. Then he set up an Asherah pole. He did
more to provoke the anger of the LORD, the God of Israel,
than any of the other kings of Israel before him. It was
during his reign that Hiel, a man from Bethel, rebuilt Jeri-
cho. When he laid its foundations, it cost him the life of his
oldest son, Abiram. And when he completed it and set up
its gates, it cost him the life of his youngest son, Segub. This
all happened according to the message from the LORD
concerning Jericho spoken by Joshua son of Nun.
(**1 Kings 16:30-34, NLT**)

The union of Ahab and Jezebel took the people into some of the
darkest days of idolatry ever known. Notice that it was during
this time that the "cursed city" of Jericho was rebuilt. The
consequences of this are enlightening; the sons of Hiel died.
It is inevitable that whenever we allow idolatry in our society,
we lose our sons and daughters, the seeds of the future!

Hiel, who rebuilt this city should, in laying the foundation,
slay or sacrifice his firstborn in order to consecrate it,
and secure the assistance of the objects of his idolatrous
worship; and should slay his youngest at the completion
of the work, as a gratitude-offering for the assistance
received. This latter opinion seems to be countenanced

> *by the Chaldee, which represents Hiel as slaying his*
> *first-born Abiram, and his youngest son Segub.*
> **(Clarke, 1 Kings 16:34)**

The altar of Baal was in the image of a bull with the head and shoulders of a man. Its arms extended outward and fire belched out from a hole in the chest. The priest of Baal placed the babies on the outstretched arms, where the child would be rolled into the fire. As the child died, the priest and priestess engaged in sexual intercourse, while an orgy occurred among the onlookers (Jewish Virtual Library).

I am a new covenant, finished work grace preacher. I am so convinced of the love, mercy and grace of God that it seems scandalous to many. But it would behoove us to look at the strict commands of the old covenant and see the heart of the Father in some matters, especially as it relates to the children, including the orphans and the unborn.

> *Give the people of Israel these instructions, which apply*
> *both to native Israelites and to the foreigners living in*
> *Israel. If any of them offer their children as a sacrifice to*
> *Molech, they must be put to death. The people of the com-*
> *munity must stone them to death. I myself will turn against*
> *them and cut them off from the community, because they*
> *have defiled my sanctuary and brought shame on my holy*
> *name by offering their children to Molech. And if the peo-*
> *ple of the community ignore those who offer their children*
> *to Molech and refuse to execute them, I myself will turn*
> *against them and their families and will cut them off from*

> *the community. This will happen to all who commit*
> *spiritual prostitution by worshiping Molech.*
> **(Leviticus 20:2-5, NLT)**

As we ponder the Elijah and Jezebel conflict, notice with me the big picture and God's sovereign plan. Just after Elijah confronted the false prophets of Baal and prayed down the fire from heaven, a national revival of repentance began. Jezebel sent a threatening word to Elijah and literally drove him into a cave of depression. It was in that cave that God revealed His sovereign plan, and it involved sonship.

The spirit of Elijah coming to turn fathers' and sons' hearts is connected to the history of the one who carried a mantle to confront and destroy the spirit of Jezebel. When Elijah finally recovered from his suicidal depression (don't underestimate the spiritual warfare with Jezebel), he was given the assignment and purpose to get up and to set things in order. This commission involved the recognizing and releasing of the anointing on young men that would fulfill the mission to destroy the evil empire of Ahab and Jezebel. Elijah replied again:

> *I have zealously served the Lord God Almighty. But the*
> *people of Israel have broken their covenant with you, torn*
> *down your altars, and killed every one of your prophets.*
> *I am the only one left, and now they are trying to kill*
> *me, too." Then the LORD told him, "Go back the same*
> *way you came, and travel to the wilderness of Damas-*
> *cus. When you arrive there, anoint Hazael to be king of*
> *Aram. Then anoint Jehu grandson of Nimshi to be king of*

Israel, and anoint Elisha son of Shaphat from the town of
Abel-meholah to replace you as my prophet. Anyone who
escapes from Hazael will be killed by Jehu, and those who
escape Jehu will be killed by Elisha!
(1 Kings 19:14-17, NLT)

Ahab and Jezebel terrorized the people of God and attempted
to silence the prophets of God. Obsessed with themselves, Ahab
and Jezebel felt no fear for their actions and would flaunt their
rebellion against God by consuming His people. They spread
their Baal worship as they attempted to subvert the worship of
the one true God.

In response to their rebellion, as prophesied, God ordained
Jehu to become the new king of Israel and destroyer of the
entire household of Ahab! When Jehu was anointed as king of
Israel, he was told, "You will destroy the family of Ahab, your
master. In this way, I will avenge the murder of my prophets
and all the Lord's servants who were killed by Jezebel."
(2 Kings 9:7, NLT)

In 2 Kings 9:32-34 (NKJV), Jehu "looked up at the window, and
said, 'Who is on my side? Who?' So two or three eunuchs looked
out at him. Then he said, 'Throw her down.' So they threw her
down, and some of her blood spattered on the wall and on the
horses; and he trampled her underfoot. And when he had gone
in, he ate and drank. Then he said, 'Go now, see to this accursed
woman, and bury her, for she was a king's daughter.'"

The war has always been over the seed. The answer is always

found in the heavenly pattern of sonship. When David's plan to build God a house was rejected, God said something profound. God told David that if he would give Him a son, God would build David a house that would last forever.

> *Behold, a son shall be born to thee, who shall be a man of rest; and I will give him rest from all his enemies round about: for his name shall be Solomon, and I will give peace and quietness unto Israel in his days. He shall build an house for my name; and he shall be my son, and I will be his father; and I will establish the throne of his kingdom over Israel forever.* (**1 Chronicles 22:9 -10, KJV**)

We know that the temple that Solomon built was unlike anything ever before. When the Queen of Sheba came and saw it, she was virtually breathless. But I suggest that she was not overtaken with the gold and silver. She was a Queen with untold riches. I believe that she somehow got a glimpse of the house that God was building. King David had provided all the materials and the pattern for building the temple. Solomon had no enemies because David had defeated them all. God told David to give Him a son, and He would establish his throne forever!

God later sent His son into our world, and according to the genealogy of Matthew Chapter 1, Jesus is listed as the Son of David. The house of God is built on sonship, with family. Jesus is our elder brother; we are joint heirs with Him. We are family. We are members of His body, not *"church members."*

I love to read and study the story of Nehemiah. He was the cupbearer cf the King during the captivity of the Jews. Life was not so bad for Nehemiah, but one day one of his brothers came and when he saw them, he asked them a question, "[h]ow are the Jews that have survived the Babylonian captivity?" In essence, he wanted to know: *How is the family?*

Upon hearing the news that the family was in great distress and much affliction, Nehemiah was sorely grieved. He was so saddened that even the King noticed and asked him why he was so sorrowful. Nehemiah's answer is very telling:

> *...Let the king live forever: why should not my countenance*
> *be sad, when the city, the place of my fathers' sepulchers,*
> *lieth waste, and the gates thereof are consumed with fire?*
> **(Nehemiah 2:3, KJV)**

Nehemiah mentioned that the city and the gates were destroyed, but notice how he identifies the city: "...the place of my father's sepulchers." He realized that his heritage was being lost.

When I see our streets filled with angry riots and homes and buildings being destroyed, I see our heritage being lost. I groan in my spirit and cry out: *Where are the fathers?*

As Nehemiah moved forward to bring restoration to the walls and gates, he chose a powerful strategy. When the enemy set out to hinder and destroy the work, notice what he did:

Therefore set I in the lower places behind the wall, and on the higher places, I even set the people after their families with their swords, their spears, and their bows. And I looked, and rose up, and said unto the nobles, and to the rulers, and to the rest of the people, Be not ye afraid of them: remember the Lord, which is great and terrible, and fight for your brethren, your sons, and your daughters, your wives, and your houses. **(Nehemiah 4:13-14, KJV)**

His strategy was to get the family units together and in the proper place. His challenge to them was to fight. The battle was not over politics or property; the battle was for our brethren, our sons, our daughters, our wives and *our houses.*

I am not inciting violence in the natural or physical dimension. Our warfare is never with flesh and blood. It is a spiritual battle for the hearts and minds of our culture. In fact, if you are not willing to invest and be inconvenienced as part of the solution, you have no moral authority to act or speak with authority.

My wife and I have personally brought many at-risk kids into our home over the years and it cost us plenty. I have seen many protest against abortion who have never made a personal sacrifice to offer a real solution to the unwed mother or the children left in the wake of a broken family. We know the power of a healthy family environment and have seen the lives of children transformed just by bringing them into a safe healthy place to be nurtured and believed in.

How ironic and prophetic it is that when Jehu came face to face to confront Queen Jezebel, her own eunuchs were the ones who threw her cff the wall to her death. These were the castrated sons with whom Jezebel surrounded herself (and with whom the spirit of Jezebel always surrounds herself).

The spirit of Elijah is a fathering spirit. We desperately need fathers that will empower sons to walk in their purpose. For many of these sons, that purpose will be to throw down the spirit of Jezebel. The war has always been about the heritage and the seed.

CHAPTER FOURTEEN

Conclusion: As for Me and My House

The journey to write this book began with a stirring in my heart and spirit - a Word that burned to be shared with others who, like me, had been abandoned, orphaned and discounted by the very people who were charged, not only with giving us life, but with nurturing us, teaching us, and loving us as the Father Himself loves. This journey stirred so many questions in me:

- How did I find my way to where and who I am?
- How did I find my way back to the Father's embrace?
- How did my journey turn from the path that had been followed and perpetuated by multiple generations before me?

I can only point to grace and mercy throughout my entire journey and continuing today, as I learn and grow and listen - a mercy that is evident even in the early life choices I made. Those choices were possible for me because of the God-ordained encounters Brenda and I had and because of our responses. I am grateful every hour that, when God called us to engage in lives in a way that I had not seen modeled - in parenthood, in ministry, in true commitment at a level I didn't even know how to embrace - we, however falteringly, said, "Yes." I will ever be grateful for what followed that yes - another forty (so far) years of seeking and searching for truth, meaning and purpose together.

By grace, Brenda and I have remained committed and in love for over forty years of marriage. The cycle of divorce is broken in our family heritage. The poverty mindset is broken. The path steeped in a lack of education is broken. We no longer simply survive; we serve the generations to come and give them hope for a brighter future. It is both our destiny and our blessing.

The book of Genesis lays out for us a picture of an emotional encounter between Joseph and the brothers who had sold him into slavery out of jealousy and spite. If we study the story of Joseph, we can see that his was not a pleasant journey. For years, he was falsely accused. For years, he was put into prison and held in shackles, always undeserved, always due to jealousy and unfair judgments. Joseph couldn't catch a break, it seemed. But Joseph remained faithful, and eventually, God placed him in a place of influence. At this point in his process, he had been given dreams, and Pharaoh had promoted him to be, basically, second in charge. He knew how to interpret the dreams, and he knew how to use the wisdom of God from the dreams to preserve the harvest and to save the people from famine, and Pharaoh had the wisdom to listen and to trust what Joseph said. This did not happen overnight. It had been, as we say in the south, "a long time coming".

And so it was that, as he carried out his role, his brothers came before him to seek help. Imagine this moment through the eyes and heart of his brothers! Imagine this moment through the eyes of Joseph! How would that have felt? What would I have done in a moment like this? Joseph had experienced the ultimate betrayal from his own brothers, simply because of their jealousy. He had every right to be bitter and angry with them at this moment. In an earthly and wicked frame of mind, he might have been justified in seeking revenge. He certainly had cause for resentment. And in this new place of elevation, he was in the perfect place to exact revenge or, at the very least, to rub his brothers' noses in his success. But none of that appeared to be on his mind at all.

His first question to them was simply this: "Is my father still alive?" So many things were missing for Joseph all this time, but his initial, in the heat of the moment response gives us clarity as to what he missed and desired most. It was his relationship with his father.

I've spent the last eight years, pondering a burning question, studying, reading, trying to unravel the answers to a complex, burning question, "God, what is this disconnection between fathers and sons that is so impacting our world?" So much of what we call evil and what we call wickedness would be healed if we weren't missing our true father-son relationships.

Regardless of the betrayal and the hurt in their past, Joseph, somehow, kept this relational perspective in the presence of his brothers, and through all of this, Joseph was restored to his father and had the opportunity to meet the brother he didn't even know he had.

In **Genesis Chapter 50**, we learn that, upon the death of their father, their fear returned to his brothers, the logical expectation being that without their father as a peacemaker, Joseph would seek revenge. They understood that it was Jacob who had mediated the peace between the brothers. So they sent a message to Joseph, reminding him what Jacob told him before he died, that he should forgive.

A good father will tell you the truth. Jacob did not deny what the brothers had done. He called it what it was - evil, but he instructed Joseph to forgive his brothers. When Joseph heard of his father's death, he wept. It is reasonable that Joseph would have burned with anger at that moment, at the thought of all the years that had been stolen from his father and him be-cause of pettiness and jealousy. But instead, Joseph said to his brothers something to the effect of, "Don't be afraid. I am not God. I don't have the right to choose good and evil. I don't get to decide to forgive or not to forgive. I'm not God." And that is how it came to be that Joseph first saved the lives of those who had betrayed him and then actually comforted them, speaking kindly to them and promising to care for them and for their families. Joseph had a level of maturity that his brothers could not fathom or trust.

When our kids were young, we wanted them to have joy and to enjoy their lives and to know that we loved them, so one of the ways we tried to give them that joy was to give them gifts. And sometimes we would give them these gifts and walk away, and before we knew it, the kids were fighting over the gifts, even hitting each other with the very tokens of love we had given them. We did not have evil intent. We did not give them anything evil. But somehow, in a certain moment, they used their gifts to hurt one another. Sometimes I think the whole world is made up of immature children, using the gifts God has given them to fight and to hurt one another, rather than to enjoy, to bless, and to do life together. That requires a level of maturity that comes to us through trials, through struggles, through learning to trust the God who is with us in our brokenness and to make choices with the heart. The kind of maturity we develop as we find ourselves hurled into unfair and unthinkable situations and have to learn to find our footing again and again.

God is forming my path; he is ordering my steps, but all he is really calling me to do is what Joseph was called to do - when I am given evil, He calls me to give them good, to forgive them.

"Forgive them," He says. "Whoever they are, whatever they have done, however they have hurt you, forgive them." For Joseph, that call to forgiveness involved his brothers. For me, it involved my father.

As I came toward the end of my work of putting this text together, I made an attempt to connect with my biological father. I felt it was important for us to meet in person, to connect beyond the ways we will always be connected in spite of our absence from each other. But when I reached out, there was no response. And so that was the answer to that - or was it?

I was awakened recently with the obvious urge from the Holy

Spirit to write a letter to him, in which I would open my heart and feelings. I had postponed this as long as the Spirit would allow. In the moment, I was overwhelmed with conflicting feelings and emotions, but I submitted to the Spirit, and the following letter is the result:

Dear Sir,

Funny how much time, thought, and even confusion and struggle I went through just to come up with the first two words of this letter. "Dear Sir," not "Dear Dad, Dear Daddy, Pops, Old Man," and especially not "Dear Father."
I settled on the word, sir, because it seemed the most respectful and honest thing I could come up with. I suppose this is one thing you can be proud of; I have a deep sense of respect and honor for men – for all men - not because of who they are, but because of who I am.

I have wondered about so many things for the past fifty-plus years. How on earth could I possibly catch up now with a letter? If we could actually sit and talk, what would we talk about? It would, no doubt, be awkward.

I can only assume that you are aware of some things about me and my life. You know I graduated high school, got married, and had two kids. You probably know a few other details, too, but there is so much you will never know. It's hard to believe or to comprehend that my life has been lived out just an hour away from your door, and we have never had a meeting or run in, much less any communication.

Even though I may never know why you disappeared from my life, I must think there is more to the story, your side, and I ache to know or understand those unsaid things. The reason I tried to reach out this one last time was to ask for your side of the story. Because my sister, your first-born, seemed to have some contact, I have tiny bits and pieces of information about you. It does seem, to me, that you did move on with your life and became a husband and father with a new family. I hope you did well for them. I hope you found peace and grace.

Until now, I never really thought of offering you my grace or forgiveness. After all, I didn't abandon you. What I mean when I say "forgiveness" is real forgiveness in a face to face, man to man conversation. I can only imagine what that conversation would be like. What would I even say? So, since that is not a possibility, I sit here putting words on paper, trying to give grace to your intentions in an honest effort.

I have to say that I am not, nor have I ever been, angry with you. I have lots of internal emotional baggage that I am just now learning to unpack, but I have not found anger to be my issue. I do see that so much of who I am proud to be has come from your absence and not your presence. My wife, kids and grandkids will never have to struggle with all the unanswered questions that I have carried; they will never wonder who I am or who they are. They will never go through life feeling unloved, alone, abandoned, or lost. They will never see themselves as orphans or victims. I have given them a fifty year track record with real history that proves to them that there are some people, some men - fathers - that get some things right, even in imperfect lives. They will never wonder or doubt if they are loved, safe, or protected.

While I don't feel angry, I have run the gamut on all kinds of other emotions. I cannot explain the empty space I sense in my life that will never be filled. I have had many father-figures in my life over the years, and for those men, I will always be grateful. Unfortunately, you are the only one this space was created for, and it will never be filled. I don't say this to shame you or to give you a guilt trip; this is just me, laying out my feelings in the most honest way I know how, having faced one more "no" at my request to have time in your presence.

As I write this, I am sitting in front of a family portrait on my wall. I cannot imagine missing out on the entire lives of my kids and grandkids. I struggle with any memories of my own childhood. I think maybe we bury our pain and trauma, and this may be grace working for us. I don't know what I don't know. I do know that my children will always know what it is like to have each other to depend on. Through the good and bad, heartaches and struggles, mountain tops and valleys, we never walk away. We would drop everything in a moment and come running if needed.

While I can't say that I am glad you left us, I am grateful and proud of the man, husband and father I am and am

*perpetually becoming, day by day through God's grace
and guidance. In the end, there are gifts you gave me
unintentionally, I suppose. Your absence and my inner
struggle have made me better. I have spent the past fifty
years determined that my family will never feel the pain,
brokenness or emptiness that I know. I have used this pain
to give me purpose and perspective. So, I close with
goodbye and farewell. I am so sorry you missed my life.
Just know that it is a life well lived.*

-Marlon

I am grateful the Spirit woke me and stirred my heart to write the letter. It was a part of my healing, and I hope it is a part of his. I cried through most of it, and I really broke when I wrote the last few sentences. That surprised me. It felt like a final goodbye.

As the months have passed since, I have read and reread the letter, and I have to say, my emotions have shifted. I was surprised, even shocked a bit when, one day, I read the letter, and I truly felt grateful! *How could I find gratitude in my heart toward the man who abandoned me and my family and who, even after all these years, has no desire to sit down with me and have a conversation? Wouldn't this conversation offer both of us some kind of closure? And yet, he remains as he has been for all of my memory - absent and silent.* And as I pondered this, unable to make sense of what for me is without reason, I suddenly felt a sense of gratitude for his part of who I am. After all, it is obvious that had he and my mother not come together, there would be no me. He gave me life. I have sometimes wondered,

Do I have his eyes, his lips, his nose, his hair? Do the hands I never had the chance to study resemble these I know so well? Does he laugh easily? Were the hauntings of his own childhood part of what kept him so far removed from mine?

Once, out of nowhere, my mother looked at me and offered, "You look just like your daddy." I don't think it was a compliment at the time, but she had no idea how those words stirred a million emotions, thoughts, and questions in me. That off- handed comment became something that awoke new wonderings in me; something important enough that I remember it all these years later, as I recognize and stir the grace of God that has covered my life so beautifully and wonder at the beauty of it as I commit to administering it to the man who gave me his DNA. Today, I feel the miracle of gratitude, as only God can bring in such abandoned places.

I am grateful for my biological father's part in my life. He was the beginning. I inherited some things from him - maybe just the way my eyes look, their color, their shape, or maybe some other part of my appearance or being, but I am here, and he gave me my beginning. His absence and my navigating around and through the gaping holes in my past have helped me to see what is needed for my own sons and daughters and even for my spiritual sons. By grace, finding what was missing or broken in my past has helped to equip me to give what I never experienced.

Because of this man, I live this amazing life. I was given the chance to find my way. And because of the Grace of an unfailing Father, I have at least a partial understanding of what this amazing role embodies. My understandings come from a perspective, not of having a loving earthly father, but of emerging out of the entanglement of orphanhood into a true and abiding relationship with God, my Father, and knowing at great depth what that relationship means. A relationship of connecting with spiritual fathers and mentoring father figures who stepped in and taught me what this whole idea of fatherhood is about, and of the phenomenal opportunity to step into the role of a father, full of wonder and even faltering at times, understanding full-well that even the mistakes we make as loving fathers are steeped in grace.

After Jacob's death, when the fear returned to his brothers' hearts, Joseph gave them a perspective that enlightens us on how it was that he could have so easily forgiven all they had done. "But as for you, ye thought evil against me; but God meant it unto good," he offered, and he went on to remind them of all the good that had come because of their misdeed. In this passage, Joseph reminds us of the redemptive power of God. What beautiful healing lives in this redemption! There is no evil anyone has ever done to me - whether actively or passively - that God cannot use for my good and, as with Joseph, for the good of countless others. This is my prayer for my life, for those to whom I have given opportunity to minister, for those whom I've been blessed to love, and to each reader of this text. This is my prayer - most of all - for every hurting, fatherless person who started life, as I did, void of the attention and affection every child needs. Yes, it is important to grieve that loss and that hurt, but let us then move into a more beautiful evolution. Look what God has given us in place of that hurt!

With Joseph's perspective in mind, I set out to look at all of these relationships with a spirit of gratitude. Perhaps, I will never understand the reason my biological father and my stepfather made the decisions they made, but in the end, what matters is the good that God intended. And in the evolution of this amazing gift I call my life, I have much for which to be grateful.

So many wonderful people have crossed my path over the years. I can't say I was seeking them; I was unaware then that some of these connections would be so significant to this journey. Looking back now, I see the grace of God and His goodness has been following me all the days of my life.

Gratitude for my stepdad was one of the toughest ideas for me to process; however, the more clearly I see myself, I can see the huge role he played in this journey to the heart of God, the Father. As I have stated, my childhood memories are sketchy. My first memory connected with being adopted is punctuated by gaps in my own understanding at the time. I was unaware that my name was being changed. I was not aware that a man had stepped into the life of a young, divorced woman with two kids and offered to love and support us. I was too young to even know what was happening. In fact, I have no memory of ever knowing myself by any other name than "Williamson."

It has taken me years to begin to understand that my stepdad could never give us what we needed because he did not possess it. He and my mother were born in the mid 1940s; they were children to the generation of the Great Depression and World

War II. Asking for and expecting my stepdad for affirmation or affection would have been like asking an apple tree for oranges. What he did give me has enhanced my life in very important ways. He instilled in me a strong work ethic. He is the reason I am and have always been tough and determined. His discipline was not often administered in love, but by the grace of God, I learned much about how I would later lead my own children. All of these things are invaluable in my life.

I have struggled to find fond memories or special times to hold on to with this man, but I am grateful that, in the end, I had the time and opportunity to mend some broken things in our relationship. He was diagnosed with ALS, and the symptoms progressed much faster than we anticipated. He was gone within two years of the time we first knew of his illness. He was only forty-nine when he passed. My grandfather on my mom's side also passed away at forty-nine. I secretly carried an inner fear for years that I would never make it to my fifties. I am grateful to have surpassed this milestone in health and with energy for productivity.

Just as my step-dad was unable to give me the emotional affirmation that I believe every son or daughter needs, my mother had the same deficiency. I am not being disrespectful or dishonoring, I am being honest. I am grateful that as a young abandoned divorcee, she never abandoned her children. She provided and protected us with the scant resources she had. I later discovered that she was a victim of verbal, physical and sexual abuse as a teenager and later the same from the men she married. I never knew these things until much later in life when we had some heart-to-heart conversations. I have reconciled all these things in my heart. She was just as broken and ill equipped to give what she had no reference point to as I was. I am grateful for those conversations - to have an understanding of the hurts that live within her; it helps me to understand her capacity for love and affection. It reminds me that we administer love, sometimes, to the best we can reach it with our own failing hands. I am grateful for her life and for the life she gave me. I am grateful she loved her children and did what she could to provide and to protect us even at the cost of her own comfort and security. I now know that she sacrificed her dreams and desires for me and my sister and brother. This is what it looks like to lay down your own lives for the love of others.

I am grateful for the many teachers, mentors and coaches throughout my life. Many were only on my path for a brief time, but I know now that their voices collectively conveyed the voice of the Father and His grace, and all were powerful factors in keeping me on the journey.

I am grateful for the Tilley family. I lived across the road from them during my early teen years. I became close with the family in many ways. The first thing they did was to invite me to go to church with them every Sunday. Mr. Tilley was a deacon, and his two sons were close to my age. Looking back, my time with their family was probably my first opportunity to witness a healthy family environment firsthand. I often had Sunday dinner with this family. I witnessed the spirit of cooperation and attention to connection as I helped with the summer work around their home. I remember the pastor and his wife being around their table often. They introduced me to Jesus, my Savior. I was baptized, and my personal faith journey began with this faith family at the center of it all. I was not aware of it then, but somehow, the Father was at work, keeping me on the path, and this season of my life was both beautifully innocent and foundational.

I am grateful for my father-in-law, Jerry. As a father, I know the experience of giving your daughter to her future husband. I know now how that feels and what it does to your soul. I don't know what he saw in me at the time, but he had a confidence to which I was not accustomed. He treated me like I was already highly successful and could do anything I set out to do. This was foreign to me, and there was no evidence to support it. At the time, we were nineteen-year-old kids with nothing but love and hope for the future. He trusted me with his most precious thing on earth, and he seemed to do it in full faith. Here we are, after forty years, and he has never flinched when it comes to his trust in me. I can't explain what a blessing it is to have someone look at you that way, to see in you more than you can see in yourself. The power of that gift - both then and now- remains more than I can convey with mere words.

I am grateful for the many voices that God brought into my life over the years. I have been privileged to walk with men of God like Bishop Larry Turner, Bishop Jim Dutton and more elders and pastors than I can name. All of these collectively over the years have greatly impacted my life and my ministry. But I have to say that Bishop David Huskins was that one spiritual father who impacted my life in a way that exceeds them all.

As I mentioned before, at an early and pivotal point in my life and ministry, God connected my heart and life with this man. For almost twenty years, we walked together in this father-son relationship. So much of what I needed from a father came from his support and encouragement. I don't even think I knew what was happening, because I did not have a real agenda. God used him to open my mind and heart to the purposes of God and the church. He was the catalyst God used to open my heart to the nations of the world. He powerfully influenced me in my understanding of the grace of God and of the Gospel of the Kingdom of God. He taught me that honor and submission to godly authority was the key to real influence and impact. It was effortless for me to serve and support him. I cannot describe how the giving of hearts to one another works, but I know what it feels and looks like. So much of who I am and the way I see the world around me and the church came from the impartation this man gave me.

My bishop, my teacher, my mentor and my spiritual father was far from perfect. In fact, during these years of our journey, he went through a divorce. This shook me, but I could not abandon or deny that God had joined my heart to this man. What I later came to discover was that my spiritual father was just as broken and dysfunctional as all the spiritual sons and daughters he was leading. Beyond his emotional and spiritual struggles, he was suffering from heart issues and had a stroke that took a huge toll on him physically, emotionally and spiritually. I am ashamed to say that I did not recognize the depth of his despair. Looking back, I see that he would say all the right things, but a deep depression was at work in his soul.

He had reluctantly taken a sabbatical from the ministry duties at the doctor's demands. As I look back, I see now that his identity was so attached to ministry that he felt he had no purpose without a pulpit. A close pastor friend of mine and I went over to visit him at his home after he had been home from the hospital for a few days. We had all the usual small talk, and he became very emotional and humble during our conversation. For almost a year, he and I had not been as close as the years prior. He and I did not quite see eye to eye about some of the developments of our network and fellowship of churches. Out of respect and honor, I never opposed him or disrespected him in any public setting. However, he and I had many conversations during which he asked for an honest opinion, and I respectfully gave it. It was a season in my life during which I questioned my own discernment and judgement. He shared with me some of the regrets and heartaches of his life that evening. We wept and prayed together, and I felt relieved that night. Less than one week later, I received a call that Bishop Huskins had ended his own life.

My world was shaken at the very foundation. August 25, 2014, I felt orphaned all over again. It has taken me years to heal and to accept the lack of answers I would love to know. I have rather accepted that he was a man, a human being, and just as broken as many of us. But I have also learned to treasure the gift that I had for almost twenty years. Yes I know the treasure was in an earthen vessel, a broken one. I will never forget how his words pierced my heart when talking or hearing him preach. I will never forget traveling with him to South America or Africa. I will never forget sitting around the table with him and dignitaries and bishops. I will never forget the conversations we had when he invited me to discuss how to handle a moral crisis or a ministry crisis. He was the voice of reason and grace for so many. Am I healed? Is all well? Probably not. But I am who I am by the grace of God and the voice of Bishop David Huskins.

And then there is this family God has given me. I am eternally grateful for my wife and children. I cannot put into words what Brenda, Chad and BreAnna mean to me. Brenda and I have now been married for over forty years. We were just kids when we started this journey. I have to say that she has handled my "call" to ministry with a lot of grace. She did not marry a pastor, much less a bishop. And even when we made the decision to "add God" to our lives - to go to church, she was not aware of my pentecostal roots.

Not many folks gave us much of a chance to succeed from the beginning. After all, our family trees had several splits due to the history of divorce on both sides of our families. I must say that it is only by God's grace and divine providence that we became the exception and not the norm.

To give credit where credit should be given, it was Brenda and not I who had the most influence on our family culture. She often had to remind me to be affectionate and affirming with the children. This was foreign to me, but I reluctantly agreed. It was uncomfortable at first, as if the words did not quite fit in my mouth, but saying "I love you" to the kids grew to feel normal. Hugging, kissing and cheering for our kids became natural. I will always be grateful for her influence on our family culture. This text has offered evidence of how many people it took to fill in my gaps in understanding of what a father should and could be. I recognize that it took Brenda to teach me what it is that a mother must be - all the best aspects of the holy spirit at work in her feminine hands - comforting, counseling, consoling, connecting, advocating, speaking truth in a turbulent moment, speaking life and churning hope in the dark of morning, so that our lives might be richer. She is a gift, not just to our children and grandchildren, but perhaps exponentially so to me.

As far as our kids are concerned, I am so grateful to see them growing and maturing as father and mother to their children and as husband and wife to their wonderful spouses. To know that they have a better foundation and a higher ceiling than we did is worth more than any personal success in my own life. My "why" is defined by my legacy, not by my personal accomplishments.

When our second born, BreAnna, read a draft of this book, she wrote a letter in which she shared her thoughts with me. I was struck by the things for which she expressed gratitude. "I'm glad you chose forgiveness and let God give you 'beauty for ashes'. I'll be forever grateful that you chose to answer God's call on your life and to break generational curses. You changed not only yours," she wrote, "but our whole family's lives. As she prepared to close this beautiful letter, she offered, "Thanks for continuing to pass the confidence, knowledge, love and time well spent down to the grandkids."

> *This is my prayer.*
> *This is my why.*
> *This is my legacy.*

Seeing my grandchildren grow up and become dreamers has stirred in me a sense of purpose like nothing else ever in my life. Seeing their growth and development gives me a joy that I cannot put into words.

Now that I am much farther down the road on my journey in life, I have found many fewer hills that I am willing to die on. I have had the indescribable joy of seeing my grandchildren begin their own journey. I have seen the ups and downs of life and have tasted the victories and defeats to which we all can relate. I think I have a little more insight into the words of Joshua as he came near the end of his journey.

> *And if it seem evil unto you to serve the LORD, choose you this day whom ye will serve; whether the gods which your fathers served that were on the other side of the flood, or the gods of the Amorites, in whose land ye dwell: but as for me and my house, we will serve the LORD.*
> **(Joshua 24:15, KJV)**

I believe, in the end, Joshua must have concluded that his ultimate area of influence was not political or as a military conqueror. He says to the nation of people he has led into the promised land, "You have to choose for yourself if you will serve the Lord. But I will choose for me and for my house." In the big scheme of things, it really is all about the family. If we build anything less than a family, we build in vain. My father had to choose for himself. My grandfather had to choose, as well. My step-father's choices, even, were impactful beyond all I can say, but their choices are theirs. As I have moved into and through manhood, I have had the guidance of a true Father; connections with many strong fathers who have given me a vision for what this fatherhood journey looks like. By grace, I have had the opportunity to say for myself, "As for me and my house…", and what a beautiful gift that is!

Perhaps that is why, at this juncture of my life, it is easier for me to connect as a father than as a son, and perhaps that is what the journey to and through this writing has been about - about seeing how I have been fathered all along - how the God of all Hope truly is a "father to the fatherless," and what an amazing gift that is!

It is no minor thing that God identifies himself as our Father. As we embrace that paradigm, it is so important to embrace the healing it takes to move us to a vision of what real sonship can be. How it showers over us, like an unexpected fall of snow. How we can hold in our hearts the fear of rejection for so long, having stirred around in our spirits all the things we deserve, only to find when we come around the bend that this Father has had his eyes on the road the whole time - watching for us. Hoping. His heart quickened by the sight of the figure coming from afar - a figure he would know anywhere. His arms spread in anticipation of a longed-for embrace. All offenses forgotten, celebration is the first thought in his mind, the first command from his lips. It is easy for me to imagine being that father.

The true gift is coming to a place in which I can see that, thanks to my Father, God, I am that son! The old lies have given way to a new and beautiful truth. What "they" meant for evil, God meant for good. What a topsy-turvy journey this has been, the last becoming first, and the first becoming last, and all of the darkness receding into Light - the child, unwanted, received as a son, the prodigal overcome by the sight he least expected or deserved - that of a loving father, running full-speed toward him, arms outstretched, tears glossing his cheeks, all of the hope of life teeming through his spirit, fully alive, fully redeemed, fully - at last- belonging in the Father's warm embrace.

REFERENCES

Alley, David. 2014. *Spiritual Fathers and Spiritual Sons.* N.p.: Peace Publishing, (n.d.).

Alley, John K. 2008. *The Spirit of Sonship: An Apostolic Grace.* 1st ed. Peace Publishing.

"Ancient Jewish History: The Cult of Moloch." Jewish Virtual Library. Jewish Virtual Library, Accessed July 2, 2025. https://www.jewishvirtuallibrary.org/the-cult-of-moloch.

"Are Stepchildren at Higher Risk for Abuse Than Biological Children?" Good Therapy. Good Therapy, April 9, 2013. https://www.goodtherapy.org/blog/stepchildren-family-parents-abuse-0409132.

Bellizzi, Keith M. "Cognitive Biases and Brain Biology Help Explain Why Facts Don'T Change Minds." UCONN Today. University of Connecticut, August 16, 2022. https://today.uconn.edu/2022/08/cognitive-biases-and-brain-biology-help-explain-why-facts-dont-change-minds-2/.

Brooks, Arthur C.. Love Your Enemies: How Decent People Can Save America from the Culture of Contempt.

United Kingdom: HarperCollins, 2019.

Brown, Brene. "Listening to Shame." TED/YouTube. March 16, 2012. Video, https://www.youtube.com/watch?v=psN1DO-RYYV0.

Caprio, Frank. "Trigger Warning." @TheRealFrankCaprio/ YouTube. May 3, 2024. Video, https://www.youtube.com/watch?v=5QjjDndPnp8.

Clarke, Adam. Adam Clarke's Commentary on the Bible. N.p.: Parsons Technology, 2000.

""Conference 2013 Day 2" WOL Ministry Church 10-5-2013." Word of Life Ministry / Vimeo. October 10, 2023. Video, 1:09:06, https://vimeo.com/76615297?fbclid=IwY2xjaw-LaoHdleHRuA2FlbQIxMQBicmlkETFRUllaQ0RReElvQjFO-eXM4AR6qxZ3KCEeYM0jXobtzJc2Q8PmSANrxJ5_s6fGEnoF-GDcQqlxAAa6L5EVCfyQ_aem_cyl4RZDYtZeQmaRozyc_vQ. Denton, C., Bryan, D., Wexler, J., Reed, D. & Vaughn, S. (2007). Effective instruction for middle school students with reading difficulties: The reading teacher's sourcebook. University of Texas:Austin.

Guttmacher. "Induced Abortion in the United States." Guttmacher. Guttmacher Institute, Accessed July 2, 2025. https://www.guttmacher.org/sites/default/files/factsheet/fb_induced_abortion.pdf.

Hetland, Leif. 2020. *Healing the Orphan Spirit: Experiencing the Freedom That Every Heart Longs For.* -1st ed. Convergence Press.

"History of the Panama Railroad Part II." The Panama Railroad. Accessed June 18, 2025. https://www.panamarailroad.org/history1b.html.

Johnston, W. R. "Reasons Given for Having Abortions in the United States." Johnston's Archive. January 18, 2016. https://www.johnstonsarchive.net/policy/abortion/abreasons.html.

Kann, Drew. "5 Facts behind America's High Incarceration Rate." CNN US. CNN, April 21, 2019. https://doi.org/20180628-us-prison-.

"Kezazah ." Encyclopaedia Judaica. *Encyclopedia.com.* (June 16, 2025). https://www.encyclopedia.com/religion/encyclopedias-almanacs-transcripts-and-maps/kezazah

Lewis, C.S. Mere Christianity. N.p.: Strelbytskyy Multimedia Publishing, 2023.

Munroe, Myles. Rediscovering the Kingdom: Ancient Hope for Our 21st Century World. Canada: ReadHowYouWant.com, Limited, 2010.

Rohr, Richard. 2003. *Simplicity, The Freedom of Letting Go.* -1st ed. Crossroad Publishing.

Rowe, Keith. "Did You Know Physical Touch Is Vital to Your Well-being?" BrainMD. Brain MD, August 4, 2021. https://brainmd.com/blog/what-is-oxytocin/.

Sabrina. "The Fatherless Generation, Statistics." The Fatherless Generation, April 1, 2010. https://thefatherlessgeneration. wordpress.com/statistics/.

Silk, Danny. Unpunishable: Ending Our Love Affair with Punishment. United States: Printopya, 2019.

Smithsonian."What Is Photosynthesis?" Smithsonian Science Education Center. Smithsonian, Accessed July 3, 2025. https://doi.org/excerpt from the Structure and Function unit of Science and Technology ConceptsTM (STC). Publisher, Carolina Biological.

Spiritual Fathers and Spiritual Sons. N.p.: Peace Publishing, (n.d.).
"The 5 Whys Method of Root Cause Analysis." NexGen. NexGen, Accessed February 26, 2025. https://www.nexgenam. com/blog/5-whys-root-cause-analysis/.

United States Census Bureau, America?s Families and Living Arrangements: 2020. December 2020. America?s Families and Living Arrangements: 2020

Vallotton, Kris. Uprising: The Epic Battle for the Most Fatherless Generation in History. United States: Baker Publishing Group, (n.d.).

Wild, Mel. 2014. *Sonshift: Everything Changes in the Father's Embrace.* 1st ed. CreateSpace Independent Publishing.

Where no translation is listed for direct quotes of the Holy Scriptures, the following version is referenced:

- King James Version